With trembling l
letter:

Dear Lori,

Forgive me fo
too many pages
talk instead? I ... to see you. I'll call you next week so we can arrange a good time for me to come for a visit.

Love,
Daddy

Lori felt dizzy. First Perry. Now her father. Soon everyone would know her secrets, and how she'd lied to protect them. Soon she would be the joke of Glenwood High the way she'd been at her old school. Worst of all, it would ruin her friendship with Kit, Elaine, and Alex. Once they found out about her father, they would start to wonder what other things she'd lied about.

Tears stung her eyes. Lori felt as if her whole world was about to come tumbling down.

Meet Glenwood High's fabulous four, the

SENIORS

Kit, Elaine, Alex, and Lori are very best friends. Every girl's ideal, every boy's dream. These popular seniors share all their hopes, fears, and deepest secrets.

On the brink of graduation and adulthood, they're discovering themselves, planning for the future . . . and falling in love. Don't miss them!

Ask your bookseller for titles you have missed:

1. TOO MUCH, TOO SOON
2. SMART ENOUGH TO KNOW
3. WINNER ALL THE WAY
4. AFRAID TO LOVE

Coming soon:

5. BEFORE IT'S TOO LATE
6. TOO HOT TO HANDLE
7. HANDS OFF HE'S MINE
8. FORBIDDEN KISSES

SENIORS™

AFRAID TO LOVE

by Eileen Goudge

BANTAM BOOKS
TORONTO • NEW YORK • LONDON • SYDNEY • AUCKLAND

AFRAID TO LOVE

A Bantam Book/December 1986

ISBN 0 553 172603

Bantam Books are published by Bantam Books, Inc.
Its trademark, consisting of the words "Bantam Books"
and the portrayal of a rooster, is Registrered in U.S.A Patent
and Trademark Office and in other countries.
Marca Registrada, Bantam Books Inc.,
666 Fifth Avenue,
New York, New York 10103.

Printed and bound in Great Britain by
Hazell Watson & Viney Limited,
Member of the BPCC Group,
Aylesbury, Bucks

To Brenda Preston, who knows that sometimes losing is winning.

Chapter One

Lori couldn't look at Perry Kingston without thinking of the time she'd eaten an entire half-gallon of rocky road ice cream, and all because of him. What humiliation!

But that had been the *old* Lori, she reminded herself. How would Perry even remember the fat, miserable girl she'd been then?

Still Lori could remember the shame, and she felt her cheeks start to burn as she watched Perry walk toward her with long, loping strides. He looked like a reporter hot on the trail of a newsbreak, she observed with an anxious pull in her stomach. A lock of shiny brown hair fell down over his forehead as he approached. He was staring at her, his eyes a dark, arresting blue.

Second period had just let out, so there was still a chance she could slip away into the crowd that was milling about in the corridor. She darted forward, attempting to lose herself in a group of freshman girls headed toward the gym. They were all shorter than she. Lori scrunched her knees down a little so she wouldn't stick out so much.

"Hey, Lori . . . wait up!" Perry called.

Lori glanced back over her shoulder. Perry had broken into an easy run. God . . . he was catching up with her! Lori's heart felt as if it were wedged in her windpipe.

She ducked around the corner, clutching her binder to her chest. What did he want from her? Why couldn't he just leave her alone? Ever since Perry had transferred to Glenwood from her old school in Morgan Hill, he'd been attempting to strike up a conversation with her.

Why me? Lori wondered. There were plenty of girls at Glenwood High who were dying for the chance to get to know Perry better. But when she'd asked her close friend Kit that question, Kit had simply laughed and replied: "Why do you think? Because you're so pretty!"

People were always saying that, but Lori had a hard time believing them. At least, it wasn't the way she felt on the *inside.* She certainly wasn't as pretty as Kit, for example. In her mind, she still pictured herself the way she'd looked before she moved to Glenwood a year ago—the old Lori who, on her sixteenth birthday, had worn a size sixteen dress; the fat girl who never got asked to dance at parties (on the few occasions she was even invited) unless someone had been dared by his friends.

The way Perry once had. Even though it had happened a long time ago, seeing him again made it seem like yesterday.

Well, she wasn't going to give him the chance to humiliate her again. She angled toward the girls' locker room, on the other side of the gym. A group of boys exploded noisily from the gym as she passed. They were laughing as they dribbled a basketball back and forth among them. One of them whistled at her as she hurried by. She felt her face go hot. In her mind, she could hear them calling after her as the boys in grade school used to: *Heeey, Blubber-Buns . . .*

Dumb, she snapped at herself. She was being dumb again. Those boys had no way of knowing she'd once been fat. No one at Glenwood knew . . . not even her best friends—Kit, Elaine, and Alex. And that's the way she intended to keep it.

"Lori . . . hey, Lori!" Perry's voice boomed out over the noise of the crowd. He didn't even sound out of breath.

Heads turned to stare. Oh, no . . . everyone was looking! Lori felt like some kind of fugitive as she ducked her head so that her long hair slid in front of her face, shielding her burning cheeks from view. She walked fast, concentrating on the pavement, blocking out everything else. She counted two candy wrappers (a Hershey and a Snickers), three cracks, and a dirty gym sock.

Later, she realized that if she'd been looking straight ahead she would've seen the door as it was opening. There was a set of Dutch doors that opened out from the near end of the girls' locker room through which a monitor could pass out athletic equipment to students on their way to the hockey field or the tennis courts. As the top half swung open, Lori walked straight into it.

The blow wasn't hard enough to knock her over, but it stunned her into letting go of her binder. Lori dropped to her knees with a soft "oh!" of dismay as she frantically attempted to scoop up the avalanche of books and papers scattered across the concrete.

"Here . . . let me help."

Startled, she looked up into a pair of brilliant blue eyes fringed with short, dark lashes. Perry hunched down beside her, sweeping things into a pile. He smiled, showing a flash of even, white teeth that reminded her of toothpaste commercials—the sexy kind, where instead of talking about cavities, they showed couples kissing. Lori didn't want to think about kissing. She wished Perry would just go away and leave her alone.

"No, it's okay . . . I can get it," she mumbled.

Perry ignored her. He picked up her sketch pad, which had fallen open to a charcoal drawing she'd done of Alicia Reyes in art class. Lori considered it one of her better ones. With a few simple strokes, she'd captured the tilt of Alicia's upturned chin, the high slash of her cheekbones, the thick plait of hair snaking down her back.

"Hey, not bad," Perry said. "I wish I could draw as well as this." He laughed good-naturedly. "I'm the all-American zero when it comes to artistic talent. Last week I made an ashtray in ceramics—what can go wrong with an ashtray, right?—well, you should've seen it. Mr. Ames said it looked more like a Frisbee that'd been run over by a truck."

Lori resisted the urge to smile. She didn't want to like him. She'd let herself like him before . . . and had ended up feeling like the world's biggest fool because of it.

She prayed he wouldn't recognize her. There was a good possibility he wouldn't, she thought. After all, it'd been a whole year . . . and she'd been forty pounds heavier then. Even her last name was different. She'd changed it to Woodhouse—her mother's maiden name—after they moved.

Nonetheless, she was terrified of having her ugly secret exposed. Suppose everyone found out what a fat creep she'd been? Then they would know she was a fake . . . that underneath her seemingly effortless slenderness was a 160-pound elephant waiting to break out. They would all laugh at her . . . just as Perry and his friends once had.

She quickly shuffled her books into some semblance of order and stood up. "I—I have to go," she said.

She started to turn away, but a warm pressure against her shoulder stopped her. Lori stiffened. She waited for Perry to say the words she'd been dreading ever since he'd walked into her psychology class three weeks ago—*You know, you look a lot like this girl who used to go to my old school. Loribeth Roberts. In fact, you could almost pass for twins, except she was. . . .*

Fat. She hated that word, even though it was

constantly on her mind. FAT. Like graffiti scrawled on a wall in red paint. LORIBETH ROBERTS IS A FAT SLOB.

"Wait," Perry said softly. "I want to talk to you. I was wondering if. . ."

"I really have to go. I'll be late for class."

"I'll walk with you, then."

"No, I . . ." Lori could feel her panic mounting; it was becoming a throbbing pressure in her temples. She cast about wildly for an excuse. "I have PE," she lied. She noticed a hockey stick propped against the door. "Hockey. I'm team captain. I can't be late."

She hated having to lie all the time, but that was how it was with secrets. If you carried them around long enough, you had to lie in order to protect yourself. And once you got started, it was hard to stop. One lie invariably created more lies, and pretty soon you were so caught up in them, you hardly knew yourself anymore where the lies stopped and the truth began.

Perry's smile dimmed slightly but didn't go out altogether. "In that case, I guess I'll just have to catch you later. Maybe we could. . ."

Lori didn't stick around long enough to hear the rest. She ducked into the locker room, breathing in its smell of wet towels and sweaty socks with a sigh of relief.

"Hi, Lori!" Jillian Singer, a girl she knew from English, breezed in through the door, wearing navy-blue gym shorts and a white blouse. "Hey, I didn't know you had gym this period."

"I don't," Lori said. "I, uh, left something in my locker. I just came by to get it."

Jillian stopped. "Was that Perry Kingston I saw you talking to just a minute ago?" Without waiting for a reply, she gushed on, "Wow, he's so gorgeous! He kind of looks like Tom Selleck, don't you think? Only cuter. I wish I had him in one of my classes. Except I probably wouldn't learn a thing—I'd just end up staring at him all period. If he ever talked to me, I"—she broke off to stare at Lori—"well, didn't you just want to die?"

"That's exactly how I felt," Lori said.

This time she wasn't lying.

"What do you think . . . the peach or apricot?" Elaine held the two lipsticks up to Lori's nose. "Smell. They're flavored."

Lori giggled. "Fine, if you want your boyfriend to think about fruit salad while he's kissing you."

"It's better than thinking about computers," Elaine replied with a laugh, replacing the lipsticks on the counter.

They'd stopped at the drugstore on the way home from school to buy notebook paper but had taken a detour by the makeup counter. Elaine didn't like wearing makeup as a rule, but Lori had persuaded her to at least try on some lipsticks.

"What do computers have to do with kissing?" Lori wanted to know.

"Nothing. It's just that Carl says that sometimes when we're kissing he has to think about something neutral to keep himself from getting too carried away. So he runs computer programs inside his head."

A dull flush crept into Elaine's cheeks as she spoke. Having a boyfriend was a new experience for her, Lori knew, so she always acted a little flustered when the subject of Carl came up.

Lori still wasn't quite used to seeing Elaine get flustered. Elaine was usually so solid and sensible. She even looked solid and sensible, in her navy slacks and plaid blouse, with her big tortoiseshell glasses. She was wearing her straight, shoulder-length brown hair neatly clipped back at the sides with plastic barrettes, the kind that came in packs of ten.

While Elaine wasn't beautiful, Lori had always admired her pretty eyes. They were an unusual amber-brown, large and slightly cat shaped, with naturally dark eyelashes. The trouble was, you had to look hard to find Elaine's prettiness, which she hid behind big glasses and plain clothing. But she had other qualities that more than made up for not being as sensational-looking as, say, Kit. She was brilliant, for one thing. Also, best of all, Elaine was skinny. Gloriously, painlessly skinny. Elaine was the type who could eat an entire pizza, with everything on it, and not gain a single ounce. She sometimes complained about being *too* skinny, though, of course, there was no such thing in Lori's opinion.

Lori's own weight was a constant downhill battle. She could gain an ounce just by breathing in too hard when passing a bakery. She knew that if she didn't stay on a diet twenty-four hours a day, the fat would start creeping on again. So, now, even though she wasn't fat, she was forever hungry. Even looking at pictures of food in magazines made her mouth water. Lori would've traded her so-called prettiness for Elaine's natural skinniness in a flash.

Elaine picked up another tube of lipstick, examining it closely, as if it were something new and exotic.

"Mocha Sunset," she read. "What's a mocha sunset? I have this image of a giant blob of ice cream melting over the horizon."

Lori pressed a hand to her stomach. "Please. You're making me hungry. Remember, I'm supposed to be on a diet."

Elaine shrugged. "You're always on a diet. What's new about that? Honestly, Lori, I don't see why you're always so worried about your weight. You look great. I mean, come on, Jane Fonda would be happy to have your body!"

Lori thought it was nice of Elaine to try and make her feel better about herself, but she wasn't convinced. She peered into the makeup mirror on the counter. Seeing her reflection always came as somewhat of a shock to her these days. Instead of a pumpkin face with a double chin, she was confronted by the image of a girl with long, blond hair spilling over her slender shoulders. Wide blue eyes stared out of a face that formed natural hollows below the cheekbones, even without sucking her cheeks in. She felt as if she were seeing a stranger, someone she would like to get to know but hadn't the vaguest idea how to get acquainted with.

In a funny way, she'd felt more comfortable with the old Lori. At least when you're fat, Lori reflected, you know what to expect. You know, for instance, that when you walk into a shoe store at exactly the same moment as three other people, you'll be the last to be waited on. The same principle applied to boys: You were always the last to get noticed, even though it was sort of ironic, since you couldn't help sticking out like a sore thumb. Boys treated you as if you were invisible. It was humiliating, of course, but at least you knew what to expect. You didn't get your hopes up.

Now, she never knew what to expect. If a boy called to ask her for a date, it startled her. She felt like a rabbit caught in the headlights of an onrushing car. She never knew how to act, what to say. The first time it had happened, after she'd lost a lot of weight, she'd been so surprised, she dropped the phone. By the time she'd retrieved it, the boy had hung up.

Lori sighed, looking down at the tray of eye shadows arranged on the glass counter top like an artist's palette. "I don't know—I guess I'll never be satisfied. I probably wouldn't be satisfied even if I looked like Shandra Britton."

Idly, she dipped her finger in a pot of blue shadow and smeared a tiny bit over one eye. The thought came streaking out of nowhere—like summer lightning—that it was the same color blue as Perry's eyes. Just as quickly, she brushed the thought aside, embarrassed. Why should she care what color Perry's eyes were?

She went back to thinking about Shandra Britton. Lori had been thinking about her a lot lately, ever since she'd found out that Shandra was coming to Glenwood High to give a lecture on Career Day, which was next week. Shandra was so glamorous. Lori remembered when her face had been on the cover of practically every magazine in sight. Now she had her own modeling agency in New York, but she often traveled around to other places (Lori had read, in an article in *Cosmopolitan)* looking for girls to recruit as models.

Lori's secret fantasy—one she'd shared only with her best friends—was to become a model. She didn't really think she was pretty enough, or skinny enough, but . . . well, if enough *other* people thought she was beautiful enough to have her picture on the cover of a magazine, then maybe she could finally believe it, too.

In this dream of hers, Shandra Britton would take one look at her and immediately offer to sign her up with her agency. Lori didn't really think it would happen that way. No, probably not. But still . . . it would be so wonderful if just this once one of her fantasies could come true.

"I don't think anyone is ever really satisfied with the way they look," Elaine said as they were leaving the store. She stuffed the paper bagful of supplies she'd just bought into her backpack. "I'll bet even someone like Shandra Britton looks in the mirror and wishes she could change something about herself." With a short laugh, she added, "Whenever *I* look in the mirror, I practically have to take inventory of everything that's wrong with me. My chest, for instance. If my head weren't on straight, no one would be able to tell my back from my front."

Lori giggled in spite of herself. "Oh, Elaine, that's not true," she cried loyally. "I'll bet Carl loves you just the way you are."

Elaine cast Lori a serious look as she hopped on her bike. "I don't know. Sometimes I think it's all a mistake. That I was so desperate for a boyfriend, I invented the whole thing. I keep thinking he's going to wake up one of these days and see the *real* me. If he ever does, he'll be in for a major disappointment."

It surprised her to hear that Elaine had some of the same worries she did. Yet it was one of the reasons they were such good friends. Just like Elaine, Lori couldn't help feeling that whenever she dated anyone, it was all a mistake, that somehow after three or four dates, the boy would realize it himself and break it off. So usually, she broke it off herself before that could happen.

There was another reason, too, for her reluctance to fall in love with anyone—one she didn't like to think about much. It had to do with her father. Because of her dad, Lori had learned all about the painful side of love even before she was grown up enough to be interested in boys.

She quickly brushed the thought of her father aside. She didn't want to think about him any more than she wanted to think about being fat.

"Do you know how many calories you can burn off riding your bike?" she quizzed Elaine. They were pedaling uphill past the shopping center, toward the cool island of shade where the town of Glenwood leveled off into rows of spreading oak trees and quaint shops. "I figured it out once. If you rode your bike nonstop for four hours, you could burn off an entire banana split!"

Elaine laughed. "In that case, I'd better slow down. I need all the extra padding I can get."

She darted a sidelong glance at Lori as they pedaled past a row of shingled shops. "By the way, how come you ran out of psych so fast today? I tried to catch up with you, but you were going too fast. What were you in such a big hurry for?"

Lori hunched down over her handlebars. Usually, she and Elaine walked to their lockers together after class. Today she'd forgotten all about Elaine in her panicky attempt to escape from Perry.

"I, uh . . . I started my period," she quickly invented. "I was in a hurry to get to the bathroom."

Lori hated having to lie to Elaine. She wished with all her heart she could tell her the truth. But that would mean revealing everything, when all she wanted to do was forget that Loribeth Roberts had ever existed.

"In that case, you're excused," Elaine told her. "I remember that happened to me once—right in front of everyone. I was so embarrassed I wanted to cry."

Lori felt bad. Elaine was so sympathetic—even about a made-up situation! A few minutes later, they were turning into the driveway in front of Elaine's house, a big rambling Victorian. The front yard was a jumble of overturned tricycles and toys belonging to her younger sisters. One of the twins was rattling down the front walk on her Big Wheel. She stopped to peer up at Elaine, pausing to brush her blond bangs out of her eyes.

"Hey, Elaine—guess who called while you were

gone? Carl! He called twice! I guess that means he's in love with you."

"He is not," Elaine replied hotly, looking very flustered.

"Carl loves Elaine! Carl loves Elaine!" Chrissie chanted, racing up the path again.

Elaine sighed as she turned to Lori. "Little sisters can be such a pain sometimes. You're lucky you don't have any."

"Yeah," Lori agreed. But inside, she wasn't so sure. Sometimes it got pretty lonely being the only one, though she hadn't felt so lonely since moving to Glenwood. Having Elaine, Kit, and Alex for friends was almost like having sisters.

"Well, I guess I'd better find out what Carl wants," Elaine said. "Probably he wants to tell me about some new computer program he came up with."

Even though she tried not to sound like it, Lori could tell she was secretly pleased that Carl had called. Her eyes shone behind her big glasses, and her cheeks were flushed. Elaine didn't even bother with the kickstand; she just tossed her bike against the huge hydrangea bush below the front porch.

"See you later!" she called out to Lori.

As Lori pedaled off in the direction of her own house, she couldn't help feeling a twinge of envy. Her friends thought she had her pick of boyfriends, just because she had so many boys calling her all the time. But that's not what she cared about. She would've traded all that for just one, a special person—someone who cared about her as much as Carl cared about Elaine.

Oh, who was she kidding? If a guy like that ever

came along, she'd probably run away. In so many ways, Lori just didn't feel she was ready for love. She was afraid of getting hurt, or worse, of a boy she liked finding out the truth about her.

Maybe it was better this way, she told herself. Maybe she would never fall in love.

Yet for some strange reason, she couldn't seem to erase the image of Perry from her mind—his blue eyes, that dazzling smile, even the yellow Windbreaker he'd been wearing.

Lori didn't know why on earth she was thinking about Perry. Or why her heart was beating so quickly. Of all the boys she knew, he was absolutely the last one she would ever fall in love with!

Chapter Two

"Do I look pregnant to you?" Kit whirled away from the full-length mirror on her closet door to face Lori. Her enormous blue eyes shimmered with tears. "Tell me the truth . . . I really want your opinion."

Lori shifted uncomfortably on the bed, which, although twin sized, took up half the space in Kit's cramped bedroom. Unable to meet Kit's tearful gaze, she stared at one of the posters—a Degas print of a ballerina bending over to lace up her shoe. The whole room was covered with posters, except for one wall which was devoted to Kit's fan collection. Kit had once told her the reason she had so much stuff on her walls was to cover up the water stains from the time her upstairs neighbor's bathtub overflowed.

She felt so sorry for Kit. Lori couldn't bear it when someone she loved was miserable about something—especially one of her friends. They were so close, and they shared so much that when something bad happened to one of them, it was if it were happening to *all* of them.

Knowing how upset Kit was worried Lori terribly. Even though she'd never been in a situation like this, suspecting she might be pregnant—how could she? She'd never even gone beyond kissing!—she certainly knew what it was like to be so unhappy you wanted to die.

She glanced over at Kit, who'd gone back to staring in the mirror. She stood so that only her profile was reflected—large breasts almost spilling over the top of the tight rainbow-striped T-shirt she wore, her round blue-jeaned bottom curving out behind. Kit sucked her breath in, then let it out, smoothing one hand nervously across her stomach. Her hair fluttered against her neck, a tumble of feathery curls the color of a ripe peach.

Lori wrinkled her forehead, uncertain about how best to console Kit. "Isn't it too soon to show?" she ventured at last. Seeing Kit wince, she hastily added, "I mean, if you *are* pregnant, which you probably aren't, it usually doesn't start getting obvious until the third or fourth month."

"How do you know?" Kit asked.

"I saw it on TV. There was this documentary on Channel Nine. It was called 'Life Before Birth.' They even showed the beginning part—you know, where it looks like a lot of tadpoles swimming upstream."

Kit sank down on the bed with a sigh of despair. "I know. That's the part that started all this trouble in the first place."

Lori slipped her arm around Kit's shoulders. "Well, you certainly don't *look* pregnant, if that's any consolation. You look the same as always."

It was true, Lori observed. If Kit had gained any weight her skin-tight jeans would've burst at the seams. Nothing could stay hidden with Kit for very long. It wasn't just the way she was built—she had an open nature as well. Besides having knockout looks, she was funny and flamboyant and . . . well, just plain good-hearted. Lori would never forget the time she'd gotten sick when her mother was out of town and Kit had stayed home from school, missing an important test, so she could drive her to the doctor's.

Tonight, Kit had called a council meeting of her best friends to help her decide what to do, and Lori had been the first to arrive. Only she felt so helpless. She wished there were something she could do to really help Kit!

Kit's blue eyes overflowed with tears as she sat slumped beside Lori. "I just wish I knew . . . one way or the other. The worst part is not knowing. It's like when you take a test and you think you blew it, but you're not sure, and when you finally see you got a D you're sort of relieved deep-down, because at least you don't have to worry about it anymore."

"If you're worried . . ." Lori bit her lip, uncertain of how she was going to convince Kit she was going about this all wrong. She thought Kit should go to a doctor and get tested, but Kit seemed strangely unwilling to do that. She felt it would be too humiliating.

Kit was staring up at the poster over her closet—this one a blowup of Mikhail Baryshnikov in mid-leap, his muscled torso glistening with sweat.

"It'll ruin everything if I'm pregnant," Kit said softly. "My dance teacher Mrs. Rosen—she told me today she thinks I have a chance to win a scholarship to Juilliard. I can hardly believe it. It's everything I've worked for." She turned back to Lori. "Do you know what it's like to want something so much you're afraid if you even wish too hard you won't get it?"

Lori thought about Shandra Britton. "Yeah, I guess I do." She thought about the hours she spent looking through fashion magazines dreaming of becoming a model. Sometimes, she practiced in front of the full-length mirror in her bedroom, pretending she was in a fashion show, putting together dramatic outfits and fixing her hair in different styles.

They were interrupted by a jarring buzz from the next room. Kit's apartment was on the third floor, so visitors had to announce themselves through an intercom that hooked up to the building's front entrance before they could be buzzed in. The trouble was, as Kit had explained, right now there was something broken in the electrical system, so you had to walk down three flights to let the person in.

"I'll get it," Lori volunteered. Kit's mother wasn't home—she was out on a date—and with Kit in such sorry shape, Lori was glad to help out. She dashed into the living room. "Be down in a sec," she called through the intercom.

"Hurry!" answered a breezy voice that could only have belonged to one person—Alex.

Alex was hopping about impatiently from one foot to the other by the time Lori reached the front entrance, three flights down.

Alex hated to stand still . . . for anything. She was always on the move. Once, when they were all kidding around, Lori had nicknamed Alex "Flash" Enomoto. It suited her perfectly. She had all the energy of a locomotive packed into her lithe, size-six frame.

She dashed inside with a breathless laugh. "It's raining!" she cried. Her hair clung to her neck in a fringe of black spikes.

Surprised, Lori stuck her head outside. When had it begun to rain? As she looked up at the night sky, a flash of lightning licked out from underneath the dark belly of clouds. Rain poured down steadily; the air was warm and sticky. She thought about the daffodils she'd planted in the front yard last fall. She'd been waiting for them to come up. This rain was just what they needed.

"Race you upstairs!" Alex challenged. She shook the water from her hair, unleashing a spray of droplets on Lori. Her dark almond-shaped eyes sparkled with fun.

"What for?" Lori replied with a laugh. "You'd only beat me. You always do."

"This time you have the edge." Alex looked down at her sodden sweat suit. "Do you have any idea how much this stuff weighs when it's wet?"

"Since when do you mind getting wet? You practically live in the water."

Alex was the star of the diving team. Lori loved

going to meets and watching her dive—a human missile arcing out over the water, all lean and bronzed. She envied Alex's athletic skill the same way she envied a bird's ability to fly—as something beautiful and fantastic she could never hope to attain. Being fat for most of her life had left Lori feeling hopelessly earthbound. She still felt that way a lot of the time, even though she was no longer fat.

"That's because I'm really a mermaid in disguise. Come on"—she grabbed Lori's hand—"let's go upstairs. I want to get into something dry."

A short while later, they were joined by Elaine. Elaine, of course, had been sensible enough to bring an umbrella, so her Oshkosh jeans and forest-green turtleneck were perfectly dry. Elaine reminded Lori of Mary Poppins, her favorite storybook character when she was a kid, because she was always prepared for every emergency. Yet at the same time, she didn't lack a sense of humor or a talent for the ridiculous.

They were all sitting on the bed in Kit's room. Alex was wearing a bright red kimono of Kit's, with her hair wrapped up in a big fluffy towel. Lori thought it made her look very exotic, and since she was half-Japanese, it suited her.

"This has gone far enough," Alex told Kit, her expression bordering on sternness. "You *can't* put it off any longer. Not knowing is driving you crazy—you said so yourself. It's driving us crazy, too. Not to mention Justin."

Kit dropped her eyes and began picking at a piece of fluff sticking out of the patchwork quilt that covered the bed. "I know, I know. It's just that I hate the thought of going to some strange doctor's office and having him look at me like I'm some"—she gulped—"dumb teenager who got herself knocked up."

"Who cares what anyone else thinks?" Alex demanded, her dark eyes flashing. "Anyway, Planned Parenthood isn't like that, from what I've heard. The place is full of d—" She stopped herself. "—Of girls who think they might be pregnant."

"I can't!" Kit wailed, covering her face with her hands. "I don't think what Justin and I did was wrong, but I hate the idea of everyone *knowing* about it . . . as if our love was some kind of a . . . a dirty joke."

"We'll all be with you," Lori reassured her in a soft voice. "If anyone stares they won't know which one of us is pregnant." She blushed at the thought. She was so far from being in danger of getting pregnant it wasn't even funny.

Kit peeked out through her fingers. "Really? You'd really do that for me?"

"Sure we would," Elaine said. "Friends are supposed to stick together, aren't they? Anyway, I haven't forgotten the time you went with me to buy my first bra. Remember?"

A soft giggle escaped from Kit in spite of herself. "Sure I do—in the seventh grade. You were too embarrassed to ask your mom to get you one."

"My mom's the practical type," Elaine explained to the others. "She doesn't believe in buying anything unless you really need it. She would've said that the whole purpose of a bra is to support . . .

well, what's there. And since there was nothing there in my case. . ." She shrugged. "How could I tell her I was sick of being the only girl in gym who still wore an undershirt? I felt like a freak!"

"I remember my first training bra," Alex recalled. "I used to wonder why they called it a training bra. I mean, what was I training them for? To grow as big as Dolly Parton's?"

Everyone laughed.

Lori stared out the window. The thundershower had passed, but water still dripped from the roof, making a lonely ticking sound as it hit the concrete three stories below. She remembered the first time *her* mother took her to buy a bra, when she was in the sixth grade. She'd gone right into a 38 B—not because she was so developed; it was just that she was so chubby. She remembered how humiliated she'd felt standing there in her underwear while the saleslady circled around her with the measuring tape.

"She's broad in the back, you see," the saleslady explained to Beth, who thought there must be some mistake about the size. It was a polite way of saying, "Your daughter is overweight."

Kit interrupted her thoughts by saying, "I suppose you're right. I can't put it off any longer, no matter how embarrassing it is." She clutched her stomach, as if to quiet the butterflies. "Oh, God! This is one test I sure hope I flunk!"

"It won't be so bad," Lori told her, even though she could feel a few butterflies kicking around in her own stomach at the prospect of what awaited Kit. "Nothing is ever as bad as you think it's going to be."

Even as she said it, Lori wasn't sure it was true, but it sounded good, anyway.

"Even if it turns out you are pregnant, it's better this way," Alex told her. "You'll be doing something instead of sitting around worrying. One way or another, you'll have a chance to decide."

"You mean whether or not to keep the baby?" Kit looked as if she were on the verge of tears once again. "It wouldn't be an easy decision—no matter what some people think. Maybe it'd be different if Justin and I didn't love each other. Or maybe it's just that I hate the idea of killing something that's a part of me . . . of us. It seems so . . . cold." A single tear tipped over her bottom lid and trickled down her cheek.

Lori wasn't sure what she'd do if faced with the same decision. She knew she was too young to be a parent, but . . . well, she also felt the same way Kit did, that it would be terrible to have to end the life of your own baby.

In a way, though, wasn't that similar to what her own father had done? By turning his back on her, he was denying that she'd ever existed. That's why she pretended he was dead. It was easier to imagine him dead than to face the fact that he didn't care enough to want to see her. Anyway, she wasn't even sure she'd want to see him now. She hadn't forgotten the shame of having a father who was drunk most of the time.

"There's no point in making any kind of a decision right now," Elaine said logically, "not until you know for sure, one way or the other."

"Saturday," Alex announced in her usual brisk fashion. She unwrapped the towel from her head, shaking her dark hair loose. "We'll go on Saturday. Today's Thursday, so that's only two more days."

"Will you be able to get off work?" Lori asked Kit, remembering that she worked at Gennaro's Pizza on Saturday.

"I'll tell my boss I'm sick. It'll probably be the truth."

"Just remember one thing," Alex said, putting her hand over Kit's. Elaine followed suit, then Lori, until all four had formed a sandwich of hands.

"What?" Kit asked, so choked up, it came out sounding more like a squeak than a question.

"We love you," Lori supplied. "Whatever happens, we'll stick by you." She was so choked up herself, she could barely speak. Words weren't enough to convey all she felt for Kit. Everyone nodded.

They were the kind of friends who stuck together, no matter what. Lori only wished she could be as open as Kit about her own problems.

Alex leaped off the bed. "Let's play Monopoly. Remember how we used to love to play Monopoly?"

Kit managed a wobbly smile. "*You* loved it. That's because you were always the one with all the hotels on Park Place."

Elaine laughed. "Let's! It doesn't matter who wins. It'll be fun."

"Maybe it'll take your mind off Saturday," Lori suggested to Kit, trying to sound hopeful.

Kit sighed. "*Nothing* could get my mind off Saturday. It's the kind of thing where you know there's no use even *trying* to cheer yourself up. It'll only get worse if I do."

Lori knew what Kit meant. She used to get into

depressions like that in the old days, and the way she'd consoled herself then was by eating her way through an entire cake or a package of cookies. The trouble was that afterward she ended up feeling twice as depressed as before.

Now, when she got depressed, she immersed herself in one of her hobbies instead. The day Perry had first showed up in her psych class, for instance, she'd gone into a real tailspin. When she got home from school, she spent the rest of the afternoon in the garden, planting a row of violets along the front path. By the time she was finished several hours later, she felt much better.

Or sometimes, in one of her quieter moods, she would lose herself in sketching something interesting that had caught her eye—a dandelion gone to seed, a jumble of thread spools spilling from a sewing basket, a cat sleeping on a windowsill. Some of her best drawings had come out of those times when she couldn't bring herself to talk about the way she felt, and so had expressed those silent feelings on paper instead.

Suddenly Lori knew what would cheer Kit up a lot more than a game of Monopoly.

"Do you still have that key your dance teacher gave you to her studio—so you could practice whenever you wanted?" she asked Kit.

"Sure," Kit said. "But what's that got to do with—"

"Come on," Lori interrupted, jumping off the bed. "Put on your leotard. I've got my mom's car. I'll drive you over."

"But . . ." Kit started to protest.

"You can pretend you're trying out for Juilliard. We'll be the scholarship committee. Please, Kit," Lori urged, "do it as a favor to me. I *love* to watch you dance."

"Me, too," Elaine echoed.

"It's better than *Dance Fever* any day," Alex said, getting in on the act.

"You guys are crazy, you know that?" Kit said. She scrambled off the bed and began rummaging in a drawer. She pulled out the blue striped leotard she called her "Jane Fonda" suit. "Completely whàck-o."

Lori grinned. "That's why you love us, right?" She was happy to see that there was something she could do to help Kit after all.

The corners of Kit's mouth twitched up in a reluctant smile. "Right."

Chapter Three

When Lori got home from school on Friday the first thing she noticed was the letter on the carpet below the mail slot—a square blue envelope addressed to her in her father's back-slanting handwriting. It was postmarked Monterey. She stared at it, feeling as if all the air had suddenly been sucked from the room.

Picking it up with trembling fingers, she quickly stuffed it into the back pocket of her jeans, terrified of what might be inside. If only Beth were home! But her mother usually worked late on Friday. She'd once complained that having her own law practice was more demanding than children, although Lori knew she loved her job anyway.

Lori dropped her binder on the flowered living

room sofa on her way into the kitchen. She noticed her hand was shaking as she opened the refrigerator door. She found a bottle of Diet Pepsi and poured herself some, gripping it with both hands to keep it from spilling. Her heart was hammering so hard it seemed to jump up into her throat with each beat.

What did he want from her? It had been more than a year since she'd last seen him. A year! She screwed her eyes shut, trying to block out the image she had of the last time she'd seen him—the stubbled gray blur of his face, his bloodshot eyes. She remembered how, when he tried to hug her, she'd shrunk away, holding her arms stiff at her sides. Then when he told her in a sad voice, that he was going away—maybe for a long time, he wasn't sure—she'd clamped her hands over her ears to keep from hearing his words.

Later, Mom had explained that he was going to some kind of hospital that was supposed to cure alcoholics. Great, she'd thought, but what about me? If he loved me, why couldn't he just stop drinking on his own? Why did he have to go away to some dumb hospital? Anyway, hospitals were for sick people, not someone like her father who just drank too much. Lori had concluded that if he wasn't really sick, then he must've *wanted* to leave home for some reason. Maybe it'd even had something to do with *her*. Maybe he just didn't love her enough.

It was easy to see why he hadn't felt she was worth sticking around for. She hadn't even loved herself back then. There was the time she'd eaten the last half of the cake her mother had been saving for company, and how, feeling so ashamed she wanted to die, she'd quickly rushed out and bought another one exactly like it and had eaten half of *that* cake, too, so no one would know. Then there was the night she'd gone to three different Burger Kings, because she'd been too embarrassed to order everything she wanted at just one. Worst of all was the PTA potluck, where she'd picked daintily at the vast collection of food, only to polish off the tub of leftover potato salad donated by her mother in the car on the way home.

Not that she'd really been fooling anyone. How could anyone looking at all that gross fat *not* know how she stuffed her face whenever she was alone? Lori realized now that the person she'd really been trying to fool was herself. She couldn't face what she was—a blimp. She'd hidden beneath shapeless clothes, inventing excuses for why she was so fat.

"It's my glands," she told Betsy Snyder, a girl in her fifth grade class. "There's something wrong with them. You can even ask my mother."

She must not have sounded very convincing, because Betsy shot back with, "*My* mother says the only reason people get fat is from eating too much."

After that, Lori tried not to eat so much. But she just kept on getting fatter. The problem was that although she ate very little when she was around other people, she couldn't seem to stop eating when she was by herself. Alone at home, she ate—cookies, potato chips, ice cream, jelly sandwiches, almost anything she could get her hands on.

It wasn't until after her father left that she really started to diet. She'd been so angry. She wanted to prove that stopping yourself from doing something bad was just a matter of willpower. She wanted to show her father that if *she* could do it, then so could he. Even when her mother filed for a divorce, when Lori knew for certain he was never coming back to live with them, she kept on losing weight.

After she'd lost twenty pounds and saw what a difference it made, she began feeling good about herself for the first time since she could remember. That spurred her on toward her goal. Over the summer, she lost another twenty pounds, and by the time she and Beth moved away at the end of the summer, just before her junior year, Lori had reached her goal of 120 pounds.

Starting school at Glenwood High was the beginning of a new life. Gone forever was fat Loribeth Roberts. At the end of the summer, she'd emerged as Lori Woodhouse, complete with a whole new identity and a closetful of size-eight clothes to match. And best of all, she found that people actually liked her! Almost immediately she became friends with Kit, Elaine, and Alex. Boys started calling her for dates. For the first time in her life, she was actually popular.

Now it looked as if all that was going to change. Lori removed her father's letter from her back pocket. She tore it open, smoothing a sweaty hand over its creases.

She read:

Dear Lori,

Forgive me for not writing sooner. It would take too many pages to explain why I couldn't. Can we talk instead? I want so much to see you. I'll be calling you next week so we can arrange a good time for me to come for a visit.

Love,
Daddy

Lori felt dizzy. She clutched the edge of the sink. The kitchen had gone slightly gray, as if one of the overhead light bulbs had burned out. Her heart was beating much too fast. First Perry. Now her father. Soon everyone would know her secrets, and how she'd lied to conceal them. Soon she would be the joke of Glenwood High the way she'd been at her old school. Worst of all, she was sure it would damage her friendship with Kit, Elaine, and Alex. Once they found out about her father, they would start to wonder what other things she'd lied about.

Lori took a swallow of Pepsi, nearly choking as the bubbles went straight to her nose. Tears stung her eyes. She poured the rest down the sink and put the bottle back in the refrigerator. She would tell him not to come, that was all. She would tell him she didn't want to see him. He had no right bursting in on her life after all this time. None whatsoever. What made him think she even *wanted* to see him?

She closed her eyes against the tears that welled up, but they squeezed out from under her lids and rolled down her cheeks. *I won't cry*, she told herself, but that didn't help either.

Lori felt as if all her lies were a house of cards that was about to come tumbling down.

"I'm not going to tell you what to do, Lori. It's your decision. It's just that . . . well, I think you'll be making a mistake if you don't see him."

Her mother sat cross-legged on the floor in front of the coffee table, sorting through a stack of coupons. Lori had seen it before—every six months or so, her mom would have a sudden attack of domesticity and pull out all the cents-off coupons she'd clipped out at one time or another and tucked away in a drawer. The trouble was that most of them had usually expired by the time she got around to using them. Anyway, it didn't matter, since Lori usually ended up doing most of the grocery shopping. She didn't mind. This way, she could make sure there was never any junk food sitting around the house to tempt her.

Beth was wearing her after-work uniform: old jeans and a blue chambray work shirt knotted at the waist. Her frizzy brown hair was pulled back under a red bandana. What exasperated Lori about her mother was her total lack of interest in fashion and clothes. Beth, however, thought it was funny that she had a daughter who was always nagging her to dress up. "Isn't it supposed to be the other way around?" she once laughingly remarked.

One of the reasons Lori cared so passionately about clothes, though, was because she'd never been able to fit into anything nice until now. Plus, despite her new slender figure, she worried a lot about her looks. Her mom was more secure that way. She never gained weight, and she had a very pretty face in spite of the fact that she wore no makeup. Lori had inherited her mother's blue eyes and high cheekbones, but other than that they didn't really look that much alike. Beth was covered with freckles from head to toe, for one thing. Lori was glad she hadn't inherited that.

Anyway, her mom was too interested in causes to be concerned with how she looked. She was forever carrying the banner for some client with a great cause, but no money. No wonder Beth was always clipping coupons!

Lori wondered if the reason Beth wanted her to see her dad was because she thought he should be given a second chance. She was a big believer in second chances.

"Is it because you feel sorry for him?" Lori asked.

"No, Lori, it's not that, though"—her mother shrugged—"I guess I *do* feel sorry for him. Mostly, I was thinking of you . . . of how bad you'll feel later if you don't see him now."

"He's the one who should feel bad." Lori frowned as she stared down at the carpet, her eyes fixing on the faded pink cabbage rose at her feet. She was sitting on the couch, with her father's letter in one hand and a container of yogurt in the other.

"I'm sure he does feel bad," Beth said. "I'm sure he feels a lot worse about everything than you'll ever know."

Lori could feel her face growing tight, the way it always did when she was on the verge of tears. "He didn't want to see me back then when I needed him. Why should I see him now, just because he needs *me?*"

She looked up and met her mother's clear, steady gaze. "You're angry with him . . . I know. You probably have every right to be. But don't you see? You've got to go on, move beyond that now, or you'll end up hurting yourself more than him if you don't let go of that anger."

"I'm not angry," Lori lied, "I just don't want to see him."

Beth sighed, tucking a stray coil of hair back under her bandana. "Oh, Lori . . . do you really believe that?"

Lori didn't say anything. She scooped a spoonful of yogurt into her mouth. It was cherry flavored, which made her think of cherry pie—her favorite dessert. Syrupy red cherries under a thick buttery crust. She could almost taste it. . . .

Oh, God, why was she doing this? It was her father. Whenever she thought about him she got upset. And when she was upset, she immediately wanted to eat. She'd figured it all out once after reading in a diet book that one of the reasons people overeat is because eating makes them feel secure. Remembering how her father had abandoned her made Lori feel insecure, so naturally it followed that she'd want to stuff her face. Unfortunately, understanding the problem wasn't the same as solving it.

"Do you want something to eat?" she asked her mother in an effort to change the subject, but also because in a weird way it made her feel better when she could watch someone else eat the things she denied herself. "I could warm up the fried chicken left over from last night."

"No, thanks. I grabbed something on the way home from the office. It was so late, I figured you'd already eaten." Her gaze dropped to the carton of yogurt in Lori's hand. "Is that *all* you're eating?"

"I wasn't very hungry," Lori hedged, dropping her

eyes so her mother wouldn't see the lie in them.

Beth shuffled all the expired coupons into a pile and stood up. Her joints made little popping sounds as she stretched. She came over and sat next to Lori on the couch.

"Lori, please, I want you to think about this seriously. Do you really believe you'll be happier if you don't see your father?"

Lori stiffened. "I don't know what you mean."

Beth touched Lori's hair. "I'm not trying to push you into anything. I just want you to be happy with yourself. That's all."

"I *am* happy," Lori said, unable to keep the tearful quiver from her voice. "Really!" she added, more to convince herself than her mother.

Beth was silent for a moment before she spoke. "You know how much I love you, Lori. I guess what I'm trying to say is . . . I'm sure your father loves you, too."

"What makes you so sure?"

"His problem had nothing to do with you."

"How do I *know* that?"

"You can't know anything unless you talk to him. Will you at least think about it?"

"Okay . . . I'll think about it."

But that was all Lori would promise. It wasn't even a real promise—it was more of a half-promise, because she knew, deep down, that even if she thought about it for a hundred years, she'd still feel the same way. She still wouldn't be able to forgive him for leaving her.

Chapter Four

The phone rang right in the middle of the TV show Lori was watching—an episode of *Dallas*. Even though she didn't like admitting it, Lori loved soap operas. The problems the characters had were always so horrendous, they made her own seem small by comparison. At the moment, Sue Ellen was in the midst of telling J.R., for the hundredth time, how much she despised him.

"Would you get it, Lori?" Beth called through the bathroom door. "I'm just stepping into the tub. And, oh, if it's Mrs. Bergstrom, tell her it's okay about her dog—the delivery service decided not to sue."

"What happened—did the dog bite somebody?" Lori yelled as she was picking up the phone.

"Uh, did I pick a bad time to call?" a male voice asked.

"Huh?"

"Your dog. I thought—well, it sounded like you were having some kind of a problem."

"We don't have a dog," Lori said, embarrassed at having been overheard. "Who is this?"

"It's Perry. Perry Kingston. From school. Remember . . . I sit near you in psychology."

Of course she remembered! How could she forget? God, why was he calling her? Lori felt her throat tighten, as if she'd just swallowed a piece of food that wouldn't go down.

She gulped hard. "Sure . . . I remember." She would play it cool, pretend nothing was wrong. She consoled herself that at least he couldn't see her so at this moment there was no chance of him recognizing her as Loribeth Roberts.

"I got your number from your friend, Elaine."

Lori made a mental note to strangle Elaine next time she saw her.

"Hey, listen, I don't mean to get personal, but . . . ." Perry continued. Lori's heart nearly stopped. *This is it,* she thought, with dread. *He's going to say he recognizes me from our old school.* But all he said was, "How could your dog bite somebody if you don't have one?"

Lori was so relieved, she burst into a nervous giggle. In that instant, she even forgot who was on the other end of the line, and blurted, "It wasn't my dog—it was somebody else's. Some client of my mother's. I didn't get the whole story, but I think it must have been a delivery man."

"What does your mother do—besides defending dogs?"

"She's a lawyer. She's very big on causes."

"You mean like Save the Whales?"

"Not exactly. More like helping people who lose their jobs on account of discrimination—that kind of thing." She thought about Elaine's father, who was one of Beth's clients. He'd gotten fired from Belker Chemical when he threatened to expose the company for polluting. Now her mom was representing him, even though he couldn't afford to pay her right away. "She doesn't always get paid."

Perry laughed. "Mine is like that, too. She's a photographer. Free-lance. She takes lots of pictures, but not many get sold. I can see why, though. Mostly, she's into this very artsy stuff—black-and-white photos of park benches and naked trees. The only thing she makes any money off of are weddings."

"Weddings?"

"Yeah—she gets hired to take pictures at weddings. You know, like the bride and groom feeding cake to each other. Mom hates all that cutesy stuff, but I think it's sort of nice. I guess I must be a sucker for tradition or something."

"I guess I'm sort of that way too," Lori confessed softly.

All of a sudden, it dawned on her what she was doing. *I'm talking to him! I'm actually talking to Perry Kingston!* She wasn't just talking to him, they were having a real conversation. A few minutes ago, if someone had told her she would be talking with Perry as if it were the most natural thing in the world, she would've said that person was crazy.

Maybe the fact that he wasn't looking at her made it easier. Over the phone, she was simply a voice without a face. Also, she'd been caught off-guard. The last thing she'd been expecting was a call from Perry.

"You're probably wondering why I called," Perry said, as if he'd been reading her mind. He cleared his throat. "I was sort of hoping . . . well, what I wanted to know was, if maybe you might like to go out sometime. Like, uh, maybe tomorrow night or something."

Lori tensed. Panic flooded her senses, washing away the momentary easiness she'd felt with him. How could she go out with Perry? It was impossible! Not just because she was afraid he would recognize her, either. There were a lot of other reasons as well. What would they talk about? He was bound to ask her a lot of questions—questions about her past she couldn't answer. If she kept her mouth shut, he'd think she was boring—a pretty face with nothing behind it. And suppose she even let herself like him, maybe too much? He could so easily hurt her again.

Lori's throat felt tight when she spoke. "I . . . I can't. I'm baby-sitting. Thanks, Perry, but I . . ."

"What about Sunday?" he broke in. "It doesn't have to be anything special. Maybe we could take a drive to the beach. Or whatever. I just thought it might be fun if we could get together."

Lori squeezed her eyes shut. Part of her felt sorry for Perry. Part of her wished he would stop torturing her with his invitations.

"I'm . . . uh, busy on Sunday, too," she blurted out. She couldn't think of a better excuse, so she was forced to use the same one twice.

Perry was silent for a moment. "Couldn't you get out of it?"

"No, I really can't," she said. "You see, my neighbor, she's got five kids. And she works nights in a . . . in an all-night drugstore. Her husband died, so she really depends on me. . . ."

Forgive me, Mrs. Gottlieb, Lori prayed even as she babbled on, embellishing on the story so that her fibbing grew even wilder. She suddenly felt as if she had no control over it. It was like finding herself behind the wheel of a car with no brakes. She was careening downhill, and there was no way to stop.

The truth was that her neighbor, Mrs. Gottlieb, had only one child, and her husband was very much alive. On Saturday nights, Lori sometimes baby-sat for little Josh when they went bowling.

"I see." There was nothing sarcastic about the way he said it. She couldn't tell exactly what his reaction was. "Well, maybe some other time, then."

"Maybe."

Lori felt bad about turning Perry down. Talking to him just now, he didn't seem stuck-up like a lot of the popular guys she knew—the kind who walked around with their thumbs hooked through their belt loops and acted as if you should get down on your knees and worship them if they so much as smiled at you. Perry had seemed . . . well, nice. Also, he was undeniably gorgeous.

A close-up of those brilliant blue eyes flashed into her mind. She wondered what it would be like to be kissed by Perry. She imagined the scene: They would be out on a date, someplace quiet like the beach. They would be walking along, holding hands and talking. When he leaned over to kiss her, it would seem natural, not at all forced. His lips would be gentle and warm, with a slightly minty taste. . .

Lori stopped herself, horrified at what she was thinking. What if Perry could read her mind? She could feel her face grow hot at the prospect.

"Thanks for asking, though," she said, hating how stiff her words sounded. She didn't want the conversation to end that way. But there was nothing else she could do.

"Sure. It was no big deal." Perry's words sounded stiff, too. "Listen, I've gotta go. I guess I'll see you in class."

"See you in class," Lori echoed before hanging up.

Afterward, she went into her room and sat down on her bed. She felt terrible . . . sort of feverish. Her head was throbbing. She wondered if maybe she should take some aspirin.

"Who was that?" Beth called from the bathroom.

"Nobody," Lori yelled back. "It was the wrong number!"

She stretched out on the bed, staring up at the ceiling. The walls were covered in rosebud wallpaper, but the ceiling was white like her dresser and the vanity table she'd antiqued herself. Usually, she found her room very restful, but now she was too tense to relax.

She lay there, staring at the ceiling as if it were a movie screen upon which the whole fiasco of

Meredith Gerhardt's party was unfolding, exactly as it had happened four years ago.

Lori realized she never should have gone to the party in the first place. The whole thing had been hopeless from the beginning.

Even then, she'd known that the only reason Meredith had invited her was because her mom and Mrs. Gerhardt were friends. At school, Meredith never even talked to her. Meredith was one of the popular girls, and Lori was about as popular as an elephant in a glass factory.

But she'd gone anyway. She even remembered what she'd been wearing: a dark blue dress with long puffy sleeves and a high-waisted bodice. In those days, everything in her closet was either navy blue, brown, or forest green. Somehow she'd gotten the idea that in dark colors she wouldn't look as fat. As if that could have made a difference!

The party was to celebrate Meredith's fifteenth birthday, and it was held in the big rec room in the Gerhardt's basement. Lori would never forget how she felt walking into that big, square room and seeing those rows of folding chairs against the walls. She would rather have faced an executioner's axe! She knew what those chairs meant—hours and hours of sitting in one place with a smile pasted on her face, watching everyone else dance and have a good time. She'd gone through this before at school dances. Somehow, she'd been hoping this private party would be different—more like the parties her parents had, where everybody sat around on couches, just talking and listening to records.

But it turned out to be even *worse* than she'd

anticipated. Since only the popular kids had been invited (except her, of course), she didn't even have the comfort of knowing that Clorissa Brody, who had buck teeth and wore two-inch-thick glasses, was sitting out all the dances, too. And since Lori didn't know any of the kids in the "in" group well enough to strike up a conversation with them, she continued to sit alone in the corner, afraid to approach anyone. She felt like a fat walrus stranded on a beach full of mermaids. She sat in the same chair for two whole hours, with her hands clenched in her lap. After the first hour, she didn't even dare move, for fear of calling attention to herself. Not that anyone would have noticed anyway: She might as well have been invisible as far as Meredith and her friends were concerned.

Each time a record ended, before another one began, Lori's heart would climb into her throat. *Please, someone, anyone . . . just one dance, just one. . . .*

None of the boys even came close to her. If one happened to glance over in her direction, he would quickly glance away. Fighting her tears, Lori watched Meredith dancing with her boyfriend, Judd Porter. They were imitating one of the dances from *Saturday Night Fever.* He was twirling her around and around, making her white skirt flare out like petals on a daisy. Meredith was laughing, her cheeks were bright pink. Each time he dipped her, he lowered her a little closer to the ground, until her long black hair was brushing it. Lori felt so jealous, she wanted to die.

The wooden slats of the folding chair were digging into the backs of her thighs. *Why had she come?* She should have known it was going to turn out this way. Tears gathered into a tight knot in the back of her throat. She forced herself to smile even harder so she wouldn't humiliate herself further by crying.

Her eyes filled with tears in spite of her attempts to hold them back. She blinked to clear them. A boy was standing in front of her, smiling down at her. She blinked again, afraid she might be dreaming. Perry Kingston! She couldn't have been more startled than if she'd been watching *Saturday Night Fever* and John Travolta himself had jumped out of the screen and walked up to her. Perry Kingston was practically the most popular boy in the ninth grade!

Lori stared. He had such incredible blue eyes. And that smile—it was so dazzling, she felt slightly dazed, as if she'd been sitting in a dark room and someone had switched on a blinding light. He was taller, older-looking than most of the boys their age. She could see the contours of his muscles even under the light sweater he was wearing.

"Would you like to dance?" he asked. He had a nice voice—not too deep, but not high and wobbly either.

Still Lori hesitated. She was sure she hadn't heard right. Was he actually talking to *her?* "What?" she asked.

Someone had turned the music up, so he had to shout. "I was just wondering if you felt like dancing!"

Her face was so hot that even the roots of her hair

felt as if they were on fire. She shifted her weight and the chair let out a loud creak that sounded deafening to her, in spite of the music. But Perry didn't seem to notice. He just stood there, smiling that incredible smile, waiting for her to reply.

"Okay," Lori said. But it didn't come out sounding like "okay"—more like the cheep of a baby bird.

Perry took her hand and led her onto the dance floor. Lori's palms felt so slippery, she wanted to wipe them on her dress, but she was afraid it might leave a stain. But from the first moment Perry took her in his arms, she forgot everything else, including how fat she was.

She was scarcely even aware of the fact that she was dancing. It seemed more like she was floating—a planet moving in a slow, lazy orbit about the sun. Perry was a good dancer. Although Lori couldn't even remember the last time she'd been on a dance floor, he made her feel light and graceful, like a ballerina. Gradually, Lori relaxed. She could feel the tension draining from her knotted muscles. Even her cheeks stopped hurting from smiling so much. She stared at Perry's cheek, which was so close, she could have kissed it if she'd wanted to. Lori felt tingly all over at the thought.

The song ended. Perry drew back. He was smiling as if he'd enjoyed the dance as well.

"Are you thirsty?" he asked. "There's punch. I could get you some if you like."

Lori dropped down off the cloud she'd been floating on for the last five minutes. Suddenly, she felt very uncomfortable. Did he really want to get her something to drink, or was he just looking for an excuse to get away from her?

"Okay," she mumbled.

Perry moved off in the direction of the Ping-Pong table, where plates of sandwiches and a bowl of fruit punch had been set out. Lori didn't know if she should remain where she was or if she should sit down again. What if Perry didn't come back? Her cheeks started burning again. She found a shadowy corner off to the side where she could wait.

A group of boys walked past. They were all laughing about something. Their loud voices carried over the music, which had started up again.

". . . I never thought he'd actually *do* it. Jeez, what a whale!"

"That Perry—he'll do anything for a bet."

They were talking about *her*. Lori felt as if she'd been punched in the stomach. If a trapdoor had suddenly materialized in the floor at her feet she would have leaped through it in a flash. She'd never felt so humiliated in her life! It was even worse than the time she'd been picked to play the part of the jack-o'-lantern in her fifth grade Halloween play.

The only reason Perry had danced with her was because his friends had dared him to. She should have known! Why else would a cute, popular boy like Perry want to dance with a fat, ugly creep like her?

Lori felt sick. There was a hot pressure behind her eyes. She squeezed them shut. When she opened them again, the room had dissolved into a watery blur. Lori groped her way toward the door a few feet away. She had to get away.

Lori didn't even bother calling for a ride since she knew her mom had gone to the movies. She walked home instead—the whole twelve blocks. By the time she reached her house, she was more miserable than ever. Also, because she'd worn her newest pair of shoes, her feet were an aching mass of blisters.

As soon as she walked in through the back door, she headed straight for the refrigerator. She got out the half-gallon of rocky road ice cream that was in the freezer and sat down at the kitchen table. She didn't even bother putting it in a bowl. She ate it right out of the carton with a big soupspoon. Tears dripped off her chin onto the table. After a while she didn't even feel hungry anymore, but she kept on eating anyway. She ate until she was so sick she really did want to throw up.

Afterward, she hid the empty carton under some other trash that was in the garbage pail. Then she went into her room and curled up in bed. The next morning, she told her mother she had the flu.

She'd stayed in bed for two whole days, just staring at the ceiling . . . .

Exactly as she was doing now.

All because of Perry Kingston. She wondered if he even remembered dancing with her on a dare at Meredith's party. She wondered if he knew how horribly she'd suffered.

Not that she really blamed him. If she were a boy, she wouldn't have wanted to dance with *herself*, except on a dare.

Some people, if you were fat, didn't think of you as a real person, Lori reflected. You were sort of a living joke. That's why circuses had fat ladies . . . because people thought they were funny. It didn't matter if the audience laughed out loud, because everyone knows fat people don't have feelings—their fat keeps them happy and jolly.

Lori ached inside, remembering how she'd hidden her feelings from others—how she'd smiled when someone was laughing at her, as if she were enjoying the joke as well. And all the time, it was as if a knife were inside her, twisting and twisting.

Lori touched her cheeks. They were wet. She'd been crying without even realizing it. The whole thing—her father's letter, Perry's phone call—it was too much all at once. She had to get away. She didn't want to think about it anymore.

She went back into the hallway and quickly dialed Elaine's number.

"Can I come over?" Lori asked. "That is, if you and Carl don't have a date." Elaine's house was only a short distance away; Lori could easily ride her bike over.

"Great!" Elaine said. "I'd love it if you could come over. I'm not doing anything anyway. Carl went away for the weekend. He and his parents are flying out to see MIT—it's one of the colleges he's applied to. So I'm here getting depressed just thinking about how depressed I'm going to feel if he gets in. MIT is so far away! Isn't that crazy—getting depressed about something that hasn't even happened yet?"

Lori smiled, in spite of herself. "I don't think it's so crazy."

"See you in a few minutes?" Elaine asked.

"Sure . . . I'll be right over."

When Lori arrived, Elaine answered the door wearing her plaid bathrobe and her best high-heeled shoes. Lori stared at Elaine.

"What's going on?"

Elaine threw up her hands. "It's hopeless!" she cried as Lori followed her upstairs to her bedroom. "I've been trying on outfits for the past two hours. I don't have anything that's right."

"Right for what?" Lori asked.

"I'm supposed to be going to this big party with Carl next weekend. His older brother is getting engaged or something." She turned to face Lori when she reached the top of the stairs. "Do you ever look in your closet and think Little Orphan Annie must have a better wardrobe than you?"

Lori laughed. "Sometimes."

She followed Elaine into her room and sat down on her bed. Elaine's room was built like a boxcar—long and narrow, with an overhead skylight instead of windows. Elaine had painted it a pale lilac, which went strangely well with the plum-colored quilt covering her bed and the purple striped Wandering Jew plant hanging over her desk.

"*You* have style, though," Elaine pointed out. "I mean, you could probably wear a gunny sack and make it look like the latest designer fashion." She grabbed an armload of clothes piled on the bed and began putting them back on hangers and shoving them into the closet.

Lori looked down at her own white jumpsuit. Underneath it, she was wearing a hot pink turtleneck. Around her waist, she'd tied a striped sash. She'd never thought of herself as particularly stylish, but she *did* enjoy experimenting with clothes now that she was thin enough to look halfway decent in them.

"A lot of it is . . . you have to find your own style," she told Elaine. "You need to find outfits that look good on you but that also feel comfortable."

She was careful not to encourage Elaine to go too far overboard, like the time she'd mistakenly convinced her friend to go all out in dressing up for Roseanne Parker's party. Elaine had wanted to impress Rusty Hughes, a boy she'd been wild about at the time, but the outfit—and the evening—ended up being a disaster, instead.

Elaine sank down on the bed beside Lori, kicking off her high heels. "I just wish I knew what my style was. Sometimes I think I don't have one."

"Of course you do. You just have to zero in on your best features and play them up more. Here, I'll show you what I mean."

Lori dug into her canvas tote bag for her sketch pad and pencil, which she was seldom without. She slipped the sketch pad open to a blank page and began outlining, with a few swift strokes, a stylized version of Elaine wearing one of her plain, all-purpose skirts. While Elaine stared over her shoulder in fascination, she added, instead of the tailored shirt or turtleneck Elaine would normally have worn with such a skirt, a full-sleeved pirate's blouse with a wide sash and a short bolero jacket.

"Wow! You're really talented at this," Elaine commented when she was finished. "I mean, I knew you could draw, but I didn't know you were this good at fashion design."

Lori blushed. "I'm not really. I just do it for fun. If you like, I could help you put together something for the party. We could pick out some material and I could make you a jacket like this. I'm not all that good at sewing yet, but I can do simple stuff."

"You'd really do that for me?" Elaine asked, her voice soft with gratitude. She hugged Lori. "You're a good friend, Lori. I mean it. The best!"

"It's nothing," Lori answered shyly. "What are friends for, anyway?"

"But you're always doing things for me . . . for all of us. I just wish you'd let us do something for you once in a while. Sometimes, I feel as if . . . well, you're holding back." Elaine fixed her with an unnervingly direct gaze.

Lori felt her blush deepen. "I don't know what you mean."

"Look, Lori, I'm not trying to pry. Really. If there are things you'd rather not talk about, I understand. I guess what I want you to know is . . . well, I'm here if you ever *do* want to talk."

Lori felt a knot of tears form in her throat. If only Elaine knew how much she longed to confide in her! It would feel so good . . . letting go of all her secrets . . . ridding herself of that terrible burden of lies.

But something held her back, in spite of how much she wanted to tell Elaine about Perry's phone call and her father's letter. She wanted to, but she just couldn't bring herself to do it.

Lori gulped back her tears, forcing a quick smile.

"I'm fine. Really. There's nothing I need to talk about."

Elaine cast her a doubtful look, but Lori knew that Elaine respected her privacy too much to pry any further. It was an unspoken code among them all. They were open with one another, but there were certain limits. Some things—especially embarrassing family matters—were just too private to tell anyone. So they never pressed one another; they just offered their support whenever necessary.

Elaine picked up Lori's sketch pad and began flipping through the pages. She stopped when she came to a charcoal sketch Lori had done several days ago of a dark-haired boy lounging against the side of a building.

"Hey, he's cute!" Elaine commented. "Anyone I know."

Lori shook her head. "He's just someone I made up." Sometimes, she sketched people from her imagination rather than from real life. She didn't tell Elaine that the boy in the sketch was how she imagined her fantasy boyfriend.

Elaine adjusted her glasses, peering at it more closely. "You know who he sort of looks like?"

"Who?"

"Perry Kingston."

Startled, Lori took a closer look herself. He *did* look a lot like Perry! Why hadn't she noticed that before? She'd almost given herself away.

She snatched the sketch pad from Elaine's hands and tore out the picture. "I never liked this one very much, though," she said hurriedly, crumpling the paper into a ball and tossing it into the wastebasket. "I couldn't get the perspective right."

Elaine smiled knowingly. "Whatever you say. Still, he was awfully cute—whoever he was."

Lori eyed the wastebasket with a small frown. Inside her head, a boy with shiny dark hair and brilliant blue eyes laughed, mocking her for thinking she could erase him from her mind as easily as crumpling up a sketch.

Chapter Five

"I'm scared!" Kit said.

Lori grabbed her hand as they were going in through the swinging glass door of the clinic. "Don't worry . . . we're here with you. It'll be okay."

Kit squeezed her hand so hard Lori winced. "Let's go back," she whispered when they were inside. "I've changed my mind."

"You can't," Alex told Kit, giving her a firm look. "You've already waited too long. Besides, desperate situations call for desperate measures."

Leave it to Alex to take command, Lori thought with admiration. She was dressed as if she were going into battle: khaki shorts and her dappled-green army-fatigue T-shirt. Actually, it was the latest style around school, but Alex didn't care anything about style. She'd been buying clothes at the Army Surplus since she was in the seventh grade, she'd once told Lori—long before cheerleader types like Marcia Connors discovered the "guerrilla" look at Macy's.

Lori was wearing her white culottes and a pale yellow T-shirt with a pattern of daisies silk-screened on the front. It was a warm day, so she'd worn sandals instead of sneakers. She noticed that Kit had dressed for the occasion as if she were going to a funeral. Instead of one of her usual colorful outfits, she'd put on a plain denim jumper that looked more like something out of Elaine's closet. She wasn't wearing any makeup either.

"It won't be as bad as you think," Elaine told Kit reassuringly—as if she'd been through this a hundred times before. She grabbed ahold of Kit's other hand as they approached the reception desk.

Lori had expected Planned Parenthood to look like a doctor's office, but the atmosphere was more like the living room in someone's house. The reception area was full of big overstuffed chairs. There were some framed photographs on the walls, and a big spider plant hung in the window.

Lori relaxed slightly. Maybe this wasn't going to be as bad as she'd imagined. She glanced over at Kit; her face was white and her expression as strained as ever. Poor Kit! No matter how it looked to someone on the outside, for Kit it was bound to be an ordeal. Briefly, Lori wondered how she would be feeling if she were in Kit's position. But she couldn't even imagine having sex, much less being pregnant.

Anyway, she thought, worrying about Kit's problem had gotten her mind, at least temporarily, off her own. As long as she didn't have to face either her father or Perry, she could pretend, for the moment, that they didn't exist.

When Kit hung back, Alex stepped up boldly to the reception desk. A girl who didn't look much older than they was busy sorting through a stack of folders. She wore wire-rim glasses, and her long brown hair was parted down the middle and tucked behind her ears.

"Can I help you?" she asked, looking up and smiling at them.

Alex cleared her throat. "We . . . uh . . . we'd like to see about a pregnancy test."

The girl blinked at them. "All four of you?"

Lori felt herself beginning to blush. She looked over at Elaine, whose cheeks were a mottled plum-red. Kit was the only one who wasn't blushing. She was very pale. Kit was squeezing Lori's hand so hard, her fingers felt as if they were falling off. Lori didn't pull away, though. She wanted Kit to know she was with her one hundred percent.

"Just me," Kit squeaked in a voice barely above a whisper.

The girl nodded. "Do you have an appointment?"

"I, uh . . . no." Kit looked as if she were going to burst into tears at any moment. "I didn't know I was supposed to."

"Don't worry," the receptionist said, reaching for her note pad. "We're not too busy at the moment. Usually it's best to make an appointment, because you never know. . ."

"I'll remember that next time," Kit blurted out unthinkingly. Then she blushed, no doubt embarrassed at admitting there *could* be a next time.

The receptionist didn't seem to notice, though. "Your name?"

Kit just stood there, not answering.

The girl smiled and put down her pen. "You don't have to tell me if you don't want to. Anyway, it's only a formality."

Kit loosened her stranglehold on Lori's hand. "Kit," she breathed. "My name is Kit."

"How late are you, Kit?"

"What?" Kit asked.

"Your period."

"Oh, that. About four weeks, I think."

The receptionist handed her a plastic cup and pointed toward a door behind her. "We'll need a urine sample. It'll be a little while before someone can examine you, so we'll probably have the results by then."

"We'll wait right here," Lori whispered in Kit's ear. Kit responded with a shaky smile as she disappeared into the bathroom, holding the cup as gingerly as if it were a bomb about to go off.

Lori sat down between Alex and Elaine on the long sofa facing the window. Seated in chairs on either side were two other girls. One was reading a magazine. The other one was holding hands with a boy. Lori guessed he was probably her boyfriend since they both looked pretty anxious. She wondered if either of those girls had thought they might end up here when they first started fooling around.

She wondered if they still thought it had been worth it.

With love, you never knew what you were getting into, Lori decided. She doubted if her mother had known about her father's drinking when they were first married, for instance. That's why Lori was scared to fall in love herself. What if she allowed herself to love some boy and he hurt her terribly? Or worse, she could end up pregnant, too.

The thought made her feel sick. She hadn't been feeling all that well since the night Perry had phoned. She kept wondering what it would be like when she had to face him again in psych class. Would he try to ask her out again . . . or would he just ignore her? The thought of him asking her out again made her go cold with panic. But, strangely enough, she didn't like the idea of him ignoring her, either. What *did* she want?

Alex turned to her, speaking in a whisper. "I'm glad Danny and I didn't . . . what I mean is, I'm glad we were careful."

Elaine sighed. "I don't think that's something Carl and I will have to worry about. By the time we get to that point, we'll both be about a hundred years old, and we probably won't even feel much like it by then."

Alex just smiled. "You never know. . ."

"If Carl ever did anything besides kiss me, I'd probably faint," Elaine replied emphatically.

Alex gave her a devilish wink. "Too bad. Then you'd miss the best part."

Lori knew that joking was only Alex's way of relieving the tension, so she didn't mind, even if this wasn't exactly the best place to be kidding around about sex.

Elaine lowered her head to hide the smile that was peeking out from the corners of her mouth. Her glasses slipped down her nose, and she poked them back into place. Although it was practically eighty degrees outside, Elaine was wearing a long-sleeved paisley blouse and her corduroy prairie skirt. To Lori it seemed as if Elaine always dressed exactly the same no matter what the season.

The girl sitting in the chair beside her put her magazine down and looked over at them. "I'm getting an abortion," she announced in a matter-of-fact voice. But Lori noticed there were tears in her eyes as she spoke.

Lori shivered as if the room had suddenly turned cold. How awful! She hoped with all her heart that Kit wouldn't have to make a decision like that.

"I'm sorry to hear that," Elaine said to the girl in a soft voice.

"I'm not," the girl said. "I'm glad. My boyfriend and I broke up last week." Her lower lip trembled. "He doesn't even know about it."

Lori felt shocked and very sorry for her, but she didn't know what to say. So instead, she just smiled in a way that she hoped was reassuring. The girl didn't smile back.

Kit came out of the bathroom. She squeezed in next to them on the couch.

"I was so nervous," she said. "I couldn't, well, you know, *go* at first."

They all sat there for what seemed like hours,

until the girl at the desk told Kit that one of the doctors could see her now. Lori gave Kit's hand one last squeeze before she stood up. Kit's palm was damp with sweat.

"I wonder if they're going to examine her?" Elaine said.

"Probably," said the girl seated on the other side. Her boyfriend was staring at the carpet, his elbows braced against his knees. He didn't even look up. "That's no big deal, though. It's what comes *after*," she added darkly.

Lori was feeling sicker by the minute. She clenched her knees together tightly.

When Kit finally emerged, she was accompanied by a tall black woman wearing a white lab coat.

She walked over to them and introduced herself as Dr. Fletcher. "Kit's been telling me how supportive you've all been," she said. "I thought you'd like to step into my office, too, and hear what I have to say to Kit."

They all got up and filed into Dr. Fletcher's office, which was really just a white-painted cubicle with a desk and some plastic chairs. It wasn't nearly as inviting as the waiting area, but Lori supposed it didn't matter so much because once you were in here, there was no turning back.

As soon as the door was closed, Kit burst into tears. Lori rushed to her side, throwing her arms about her.

"Oh, Kit . . . I'm so sorry!" she cried. "I was really hoping it would turn out that you weren't pregnant!"

Kit lifted her head, swiping at her wet cheeks

with the heels of her palms. "I'm not!" she said. "The test came out negative! I'm just so relieved . . . I . . . I don't know what came over me."

Suddenly, Alex and Elaine were crowding over to hug her, too.

Alex cried, "You really had us worried!"

"Not to mention scared out of our wits!" Elaine put in.

The only one who wasn't smiling was Dr. Fletcher. "You were very lucky this time," she said. Lori noticed she was wearing big silver hoop earrings. They swung back and forth when she sat down on the edge of her desk.

Kit ducked her head sheepishly. "I . . . I guess we weren't as careful as we should have been."

Dr. Fletcher sighed. "Unfortunately, you're not the only one. You girls—you want to grow up in such a hurry! Well, okay, that's your choice, but that also means taking the responsibilities of being an adult as well. A lot of girls don't want to admit they're having sex. Not even to themselves. Now"—she held up a hand—"I'm not presuming that all of you are sexually active. I'm just saying that if you are—or even if you're just thinking about it—don't wait until it's too late to face up to the *facts*. Not only for your sake but for your boyfriend's and family's sakes as well."

Lori felt embarrassed, even though she knew Dr. Fletcher wasn't really being mean. She probably just didn't want to see them end up like those other girls out in the waiting area.

After giving them a little lecture about the different kinds of birth control that were available, Dr.

Fletcher gave each a pamphlet on the subject. Lori glanced through it quickly, then shoved it out of sight into her purse. She noticed that Elaine and Alex were still busy looking at their pamphlets.

Finally, Alex looked up and said, "There's one thing I don't get. How come it's so one-sided? I mean, look at this pamphlet. There's got to be eighty zillion different kinds of birth control for women, and only *one* that I know of for men. It doesn't seem fair that girls get stuck with most of the responsibility."

"That's true," Dr. Fletcher said, giving in to a small smile. "But you'll have to take up that gripe with Mother Nature. The plain truth is that it's a lot easier not to worry about something when you're not the one who has to pay the consequences."

"I wonder what it would be like if boys could get pregnant," Elaine said.

Dr. Fletcher laughed. "Now *that* would be something!" When she saw them to the door, she was still grinning. "Good-bye, girls."

Lori was so relieved to be out of there, she broke into a skipping run as soon as they hit the parking lot. Alex caught up with her, letting out a loud whoop.

"Wow, I feel like I just got let out of prison!" she shouted.

Kit laughed. "What about me? I could've ended up with a life sentence." She sobered as they all climbed into Alex's battered green Dodge. "You know, I used to think babies were just cute and cuddly until I started baby-sitting. Remember when Mrs. Jeffries had her baby? Well, I took care of it once after she brought it home from the hospital. It was so tiny, it could've fit into a shoe box. But, boy, was it a lot of trouble! I couldn't sit down for a minute. Then it threw up all over my brand-new sweater. That's when I decided I'd probably wait until I was about forty before I have a baby. I can't *believe* how I almost blew it!"

"Well, it *is* sort of a problem," Alex admitted as she was turning out of the parking lot. It was hot inside the car, so she rolled down her window. Lori, seated in the back seat beside Elaine, was caught in a blast of warm air. "I mean, there you are feeling all romantic when suddenly, right in the middle of it, one of you has to get up and start fumbling around. It sort of spoils the mood."

"I'm beginning to see there are certain advantages to just fantasizing about sex instead of actually doing it," Elaine said.

"Like what?" Alex wanted to know.

"Like not having to worry about birth control."

"I wonder if our parents forgot about birth control when they had us," Lori mused aloud. She was thinking mostly of her father, wondering if he'd ever wanted her, even back in the beginning.

"Not *my* parents," Alex replied emphatically. "My mother is so organized she could go grocery shopping in her sleep and not forget anything. My father's the same way, only with him it's golf balls. He plays golf every Sunday, and he's never lost one yet. He prides himself on it."

"I don't think having babies is the same as grocery shopping and golf balls," Elaine said.

"My mother didn't want me," Kit said bluntly.

"Not right at first, anyway. She told me so herself. The way she tells it, she got sort of attached to the idea of having me when I started kicking up a fuss inside her. Then by the time I was born, she was pretty excited about the whole thing."

Lori wondered what it would be like having a mother like Kit's. People were always mistaking them for sisters. Janice was young-looking and very pretty, like Kit. She even acted young and, at times, flirtatious. According to Kit, she'd had lots of boyfriends since her divorce from Kit's father, but hadn't yet found "Mr. Right." Kit's theory was that her mother, deep down, was afraid of love, because loving someone meant opening yourself up to the possibility of getting hurt. If that was so, Lori didn't blame Janice. Actually, she felt pretty much the same way herself.

She doubted she would ever fall in love with anybody. Or that anybody would really fall in love with her. Real love, she thought, wasn't the same as having a crush on someone, like the one she'd had on Mr. Castellano last semester. If you really loved someone, you had to love the way they were on the *inside*, not just the way they looked on the outside.

Well, she wasn't going to fall in love so it didn't matter, she told herself.

Anyway, Lori was sure that if any boy ever discovered the truth about her—the "real" Lori that was beneath the snowdrift of lies—he wouldn't want to stay involved with her for long.

"I feel like celebrating," Kit said. "How about it—ice cream sundaes, on me?"

"Great," Elaine said. "I need something to cool me

off after all that. I was so nervous back there, I really worked up a sweat."

"Me, too," Alex put in. "I feel like I've been through the Boston Marathon!"

When they reached the mall, she pulled up in front of Swensen's Ice Cream Parlor. They all trooped inside. Alex and Elaine both ordered double scoops. Kit splurged on a hot fudge sundae, complete with chopped nuts and baby marshmallows.

"I may end up having to wear maternity clothes after all," she kidded, spooning up a blob of whipped cream.

Lori wasn't going to have anything, but she finally gave in and ordered a small cone of orange sherbet.

"I really shouldn't be doing this," she said, feeling slightly guilty as she twirled it against her tongue.

"Forget it," Alex said. "You don't need to diet anymore, Lori. You're already skinny enough to be a model."

Lori looked up from her ice-cream cone. "You really think so?" Alex's opinion really counted with her, since she usually said what she was really thinking. At times, her frankness bordered on brutal honesty.

"You're the only one who *doesn't* think so," Elaine said. "But I'll bet if you ever saw a really good picture of yourself, you'd know what we were talking about."

"You should put together a portfolio," Kit suggested, pausing between bites. "That's what my cousin did. If you want to be a model, Renee says the first step is to get a professional photographer to take a whole bunch of pictures of you. Then you show them to modeling agencies so they can see how photogenic you are."

"What if I'm not photogenic enough?" Lori asked doubtfully. She had actually been thinking about putting together a portfolio . . . but she hadn't gotten up the nerve yet. What if the agency said she wasn't pretty enough? Or skinny enough? Or both?

They were sitting outside, at a wrought-iron table facing the garden in the center of the mall. After they'd finished their ice cream, Alex seized her without warning by the hand. "Come on, let's find out!"

"What are you talking about? Hey, wait a minute!"

Lori made a weak stab at trying to get away, but Alex's grip around her wrist was like iron. Alex tugged her across the mall, in the direction of Woolworth's. She glanced back over her shoulder.

"Help!" she cried out in mock distress. "I'm being kidnapped!" But Kit and Elaine, bringing up the rear, only smiled.

When they got to Woolworth's, Alex steered her toward the instant photo booth in back, where you could get a strip of four snapshots for two dollars. Kit and Elaine crowded in, too. Alex shoved a handful of quarters into the slot.

"Say cheese!" she commanded.

But they were all giggling too hard to hold a straight face. They laughed even harder when the pictures came out. In one, Kit had her tongue sticking out. All you could see of Elaine was her glasses. Alex had her head thrown back, resting against Lori's shoulder.

"I look like a chipmunk," Lori groaned. "How come my cheeks look so puffy?"

"It's only because you're laughing," Kit said, peering over her shoulder to have a look. "Most people *do* look like that when they're laughing. Look at me!"

"All I can see is your tongue."

Alex giggled. "Once Danny and I took these pictures of ourselves kissing. Wow, was it gross-looking! If I didn't know how good it felt, I'd never want to try it."

"I think you look great in these pictures," Elaine told Lori. "Better than Cheryl Tiegs."

"I think you need new glasses." Lori laughed.

They browsed around the store for the next half hour or so. Elaine bought a shower cap and a package of Bic pens. While she was standing in line at the checkout counter, Kit went to phone Justin, who was still at work, to tell him the good news.

"What did he say?" Lori wanted to know when Kit had emerged from the phone booth, grinning.

"He said he never thought he'd be so excited about *not* being a father." Kit laughed. "I asked him if he was planning on handing out cigars."

Lori was glad that everything had turned out so well for Kit. Maybe there really was such a thing as a happy ending.

For her own sake, as well, she hoped so.

"Let's go over to the Emporium," Lori suggested after they'd toured every aisle in Woolworth's. She turned to Elaine. "We could get some material for that jacket I'm going to make you."

They were passing through Junior Fashions on the first floor of the Emporium when Lori spotted a blouse that would go perfectly with the jacket she planned on making for Elaine. It was low necked, with long full sleeves, and was made of a light silky fabric in a soft rose color. It was plain enough to suit Elaine's taste, yet it was so feminine Lori was sure Carl would love it.

She stopped to show it to Elaine. "You could wear it with practically anything," she pointed out. "And it's on sale. Only fourteen dollars."

"It is pretty." Elaine fingered the price tag thoughtfully. "I'm just not sure it's really me."

Alex nudged her toward the dressing room. "Try it on. I bet it'll look fantastic on you."

More to keep Elaine company than anything else, they each grabbed something off the rack to try on in the dressing room. Elaine and Kit took the empty cubicle in the front; Alex and Lori found one in the back.

While Alex struggled with the zippers on a yellow jumpsuit Lori slipped into the outfit she'd picked out—an Ultrasuede miniskirt with a matching vest.

"I don't know," she said, eyeing herself critically in the mirror. "Don't you think it makes my legs look fat?"

"Don't be silly—you look fabulous," Alex argued emphatically. She crowded in beside Lori at the mirror.

"So do you," Lori said with a giggle, admiring Alex

in her yellow jumpsuit. "The only thing missing is the parachute."

A saleswoman poked her head into their cubicle. "Need any help, girls?"

"My friend thinks this outfit makes her look fat," Alex spoke up with her usual candor. "Maybe if *you* tell her how good it looks, she'll believe it."

Lori shot Alex a dirty look, which Alex totally ignored.

The saleswoman—a short, plump woman with stiff blond hair—stepped inside to get a closer look. She gave a wistful sigh, and said, "Just like a model! What I would give for a figure like yours, dear." Lori didn't know what to say. She was both pleased and embarrassed.

"She's going to be a model someday," Alex piped, ignoring the elbow Lori was digging into her side.

The woman brightened. "Maybe you'd like to model for us, in that case. We're having a big fashion show the Saturday after next. We could use an extra model."

Lori lowered her gaze, staring down at the floor. She didn't know what to think. Part of her felt so uncomfortable, she wanted to run away, but at the same time, she was flattered beyond belief. Somebody—a complete stranger—thought she could be a model!

"I . . . I don't know," she stammered. "I'm not sure I can."

The woman smiled reassuringly. "Well, when you decide, you can call and let me know. Just ask for Mrs. Pollard. That's me, and I'm in charge."

"Thanks," Lori mumbled, her cheeks burning. "I will."

Alex pounced on her the minute Mrs. Pollard left. "Why didn't you say yes?" she hissed. "Think what a great chance it could be! Why did you tell her you weren't sure?"

Lori felt so confused, her head was spinning. She slumped down on the bench beside the mirror. "I don't know," she said.

She honestly didn't.

Chapter Six

Lori dreaded going to school on Monday morning. It wasn't that she hated school, only that she was nervous about seeing Perry. He sat two seats away from her in psych. Suppose he asked her out again? What kind of excuse could she use this time?

"I hope he ignores me," she said aloud to her reflection in the round mirror over her vanity table as she was brushing her hair.

But she didn't really mean it. For some reason, the thought of Perry ignoring her left her feeling strangely hollow inside. It was crazy! How could she feel this way about something turning out exactly the way she'd wanted it to?

Maybe it was because Perry had sounded so nice

over the phone. He'd been so easy to talk to, not like Ben Price, or some of the other boys who sometimes called her. Ben always got tongue-tied whenever he tried to talk to her, which only made Lori feel more self-conscious than she already was. She hated those embarrassing silences. But what she hated even worse was how boys like Ben acted when they asked her out—as if she'd be doing them a big favor by saying yes.

Lori dreamed of having a boyfriend who wouldn't treat her as if she were a Barbie doll . . . or some kind of conquest—someone who cared about her as a person and who was more concerned with how she felt about things than how she looked—someone who would understand about her father, for instance.

There were times, she decided, when being thought of as pretty was just as difficult to deal with as being fat.

Lori had home ec first period. During class, she had a hard time concentrating on what she was supposed to be doing—sewing a zipper into the skirt she was making. Near the end of the period, she discovered she'd sewn it in the wrong way. She had no choice but to rip it out and start all over again.

She got to her psych class just after the second bell rang. She slid into her seat near the back before Mrs. Wiseman, who was writing something on the board, could notice she was late. Mrs. Wiseman was the old-fashioned type who believed in tardy slips, Lori had learned from experience.

Breathing a sigh of relief, she glanced over at

Elaine seated at the desk beside her. Elaine winked, making a circle with her thumb and forefinger to signal "you made it."

Lori's gaze wandered over to where Perry was sitting. Her heart beat a little faster. She wished he weren't so good-looking! He was slouched down in his chair with his long legs stretched out in front, the heels of his sneakers resting on the rungs of the chair in front of him. She noticed there was a tiny rip in his T-shirt, just below the shoulder, where the material stretched across the tanned swell of his muscles. For some crazy reason, she found she had an irresistible urge to go over and wiggle her finger through that hole. She grew embarrassed at the thought.

Then Perry must have felt her staring, because he looked around as if someone had tapped him on the shoulder. Lori quickly looked away. She stared straight at the blackboard, as if fascinated by the homework assignment Mrs. Wiseman was writing down. All of a sudden the room seemed very warm.

Mrs. Wiseman's lecture actually turned out to be fairly interesting for a change, though Lori was still having trouble concentrating. It was all about the psychological effects of deprivation on babies. Halfway through the period, she unexpectedly called on Lori.

"Miss Woodhouse, could you tell us please, what a Skinner Box is? If you read Friday's homework assignment, you should know."

Lori felt a flash of heat rise in her cheeks. Her throat tightened. Out of the corner of her eye, she saw Perry staring at her. He wasn't the only one. A few heads in front turned around to look at her, too.

"I don't know," she mumbled.

The worst part was, she *did* know the answer. But it wasn't the kind of question you could answer in one quick sentence, and the thought of the whole class—especially Perry—staring at her while she struggled through a long explanation seemed too much to bear. It was better to have Mrs. Wiseman think she hadn't done her homework.

As soon as the bell rang, Lori darted out into the hallway. She'd forgotten about waiting for Elaine, and was halfway to her locker before Elaine caught up.

"What did you do that for?" Elaine asked when she'd caught her breath.

She peered at Lori curiously through her glasses. Her shoulder-length brown hair was scooped back in a ponytail, and she was wearing her favorite green turtleneck tucked into corduroy jeans.

"What do you mean?" Lori asked.

"You knew the answer to that question. You told me you read the homework assignment. Why did you tell Mrs. Wiseman you didn't know?"

Lori hung her head, letting her long hair slip in front of her face. "I guess I just forgot. My brain sort of goes on strike whenever there's a bunch of people staring at me."

"You mean, like Perry Kingston, for instance?"

Lori felt so flustered, she hardly knew where she was going. Elaine had to grab her elbow to keep her from plowing into a kiosk. Why did Elaine always have to be so darn smart about everything? Lori wondered.

Still, she hedged. "Perry has nothing to do with it."

"Oh come on, Lori. I saw the way you were looking over at him. Besides, I happen to know for a fact that he was going to call you up, because he asked me for your phone number on Friday. I didn't think you'd mind me giving it to him, since he could've just as easily looked it up in the phone book. So, did he call?"

Lori nodded. She stopped at her locker and began twirling the combination nervously.

"Well," Elaine urged, "Aren't you going to tell me how it went? I know it's probably not such a big deal to you when a boy calls, not the way it would be to me, but still . . ."

"It was nothing much," Lori said. "He asked me out, that's all."

"Nothing!" Elaine's amber-brown eyes widened in astonishment. "Practically the cutest boy in the whole school asks you out, and you say it's *nothing*. Lori, have you gone bananas? Perry's about the neatest guy I've ever seen. Up close in person, that is. Not counting the movies. Just don't tell Carl I said so."

Lori thought so, too, only she didn't dare reveal how she felt about Perry. The whole thing was too complicated. If she tried to explain her feelings for him, she would have to start from the beginning and explain *everything*. She had a fleeting image of all her lies unraveling like a giant ball of yarn.

"That's just it," she said. She opened her locker and began rummaging around for her Spanish notebook. "Perry's so neat-looking, he's probably been on a thousand dates. I just didn't feel like being number one thousand and one. It would be sort of like standing in line at the cafeteria."

"He actually asked you out!" Elaine grabbed her by the shoulder.

Lori found her notebook and slammed her locker shut. "It was no big deal," she lied.

"Easy for you to say. I probably would've passed out on the spot. What did you tell him?"

"I told him I was busy."

"He probably thinks the same thing about you that you do about him—that you've got thousands of boyfriends."

A lot of people thought that, Lori knew, but it wasn't true. Last year, there was this boy in her English class, Rick Lewis, a senior whom she had a secret crush on. She'd really wanted Rick to ask her out, and once it even seemed as if he was on the verge of doing so, but he never did. Recently, she'd run into him at the mall. He was home from college on semester break. They had a cup of coffee together and Rick admitted he'd wanted to ask her out, but had never gotten up the courage. He was so sure she already had more boyfriends than she knew what to do with.

If every boy felt the way Rick had, Lori realized, she would never have *any* dates! As it was, she'd gone out with only three boys since the beginning of the year. And even then, none of them had any real romance potential.

"Well, that proves it then," Lori said.

"What?"

Elaine fell into step beside Lori as she walked

toward her next class. They both had classes in the same building during third period.

"That Perry didn't really mean anything by asking me out. If he already has a zillion girl friends, and he thinks I've got just as many boyfriends, then he couldn't be interested in anything that serious. It was probably just a spur-of-the-moment thing."

Elaine didn't seem convinced. "I wouldn't be too sure of that if I were you. The way Perry *looks* at you in class when you're not looking . . ."

Lori could feel herself growing flustered. Her face felt tight and hot. It was strange how she felt—both panic-stricken and pleased at the same time.

"Really?" she asked, clutching her binder tightly against her chest. "He does?" She smoothed her hair back over one ear.

"All the time. If he spent as much time studying the blackboard as he does your face, he'd probably be getting straight A's in that class!"

Lori struggled against her emotions. Probably the only reason Perry was staring at her, she told herself, was because he was trying to figure out where he knew her from.

"I hate it when someone does that," Lori countered. "You wonder if they're staring at you for a reason. Like maybe you have a piece of lettuce stuck between your teeth, or there's some hideous zit on your forehead."

Elaine was silent for a moment, then she said, pointedly, "I don't think that's it with Perry. Take the Mona Lisa, for instance. You don't have to have a reason to want to stare at it. You just do—because, well, it's compelling."

Lori didn't know what to say to that. People were always speculating on the reason Mona Lisa was smiling. Maybe she'd had her secrets as well. Maybe she'd once been a blimp and was smiling because no one would know it to look at her.

The second bell rang just as Lori reached her classroom. Third period she had Spanish, with Mr. Marquez. It wasn't one of her hardest classes, since he spent most of the time talking about food. He was very fat and loved to cook, mostly Italian and French food. Lori liked being in Mr. Marquez's class, even though she wasn't learning very much Spanish.

"See you at lunch," Lori called as she was going in.

Elaine waved good-bye. "See you at lunch." Her mouth turned up in a mischievous smile. "Mona Lisa!"

"It's so incredible, I can hardly believe it!" Kit sighed as she sank down on the bleachers beside her three friends.

They were eating lunch out on the bleachers overlooking the football field. Alex maintained that watching the football team's spring practice was more fun than eating any day. Lori didn't care so much about football practice, but the weather was so warm and sunny she couldn't resist the opportunity to sit outdoors.

"My dance teacher, Mrs. Rosen, called last night to say she wants to do a videotape of me," Kit went on, "to send to Juilliard. She really thinks I have a good chance at a scholarship."

It was no surprise to Lori that Kit's teacher considered her an excellent dancer, but she was glad to see Kit so excited about her future now that the threat of pregnancy no longer hung over her. Lori bit into her hard-boiled egg. She wished her own plans for the future weren't so half-baked.

It worried her that she didn't know exactly what she was going to do after she graduated. She'd applied to a few state colleges, but what she really wanted to do was to become a model. Only that wasn't something you could just decide to be all by yourself, she knew.

Tomorrow was Senior Career Day. Instead of regular classes there would be seminars. Each seminar would be held by a professional in that particular field. You were allowed to choose two. Lori had signed up first for the one on modeling, which was being given by Shandra Britton. She wasn't the only one, though; practically every other girl in the senior class had signed up, too.

The second seminar she'd signed up for was on Social Work. Lori wasn't sure exactly why she'd signed up for that one, except that she'd always liked the idea of having a job where she could help other people. Probably, she'd gotten that from her mother. Social work wasn't as glamorous as modeling, but probably it was very rewarding in its own way.

Lori was jolted from her thoughts when Elaine said to Kit, "Hey, maybe you could make one of those videos like you see on MTV." She laughed. "You could even use special effects to jazz it up. Wear a sequined leotard and throw in some fireworks."

"I don't think Juilliard would be very impressed

by sequins and fireworks," Kit answered with a giggle. "I think I'll play it straight this time."

"I can hardly believe this is our last year," Alex said wistfully. She leaned forward on her elbows, staring out at the field. "Pretty soon it'll be summer, then we'll be going to college. I wonder what our lives will be like a year from now?"

"Hey, don't rush it," Elaine said quickly. "I'm in no hurry for the spring to end."

Lori felt a strange thickness in her chest. She would really miss her friends after graduation. Suddenly she realized how much she depended on them; how much she loved them—Kit, Alex, and Elaine—they were more than friends, they were *part* of her.

She looked over at Alex in her khaki pants and rainbow suspenders, her hair tucked up underneath a bright red beret. Alex had all the courage she'd always wished for in herself. Just being around Alex gave her strength.

And Kit—well, what *couldn't* you say about Kit? She was generosity itself. Sitting there in her Hawaiian-print dress, a bright ribbon woven through her sunburst of golden curls, she practically shone. No one near Kit could possibly fail to be dazzled by her looks, or warmed by her kindness.

And, of course, there was Elaine. Sensitive, loyal, supportive. Half of Elaine's smartness, Lori thought, was in the way she related to people. She knew how to treat people, how to make them feel good about themselves.

Lori felt a bubble of panic rise inside her as she tried to envision the day when she would be apart from her friends. What would she do without them? How could she ever manage on her own? Tears pricked her eyes, and she quickly looked away so her friends wouldn't ask why she was crying.

She stared out over the sprawling green field, watching a group of boys as they tossed a football back and forth among themselves, shouting and laughing. They were too far away for her to see their faces, but then one of them called out loudly, "Hey, Kingston, over here!"

Lori peered more closely, recognizing the tall, dark-haired figure as Perry. From this safe distance, she could watch him comfortably without being afraid that he would watch her back. She took in the easy graceful way he loped across the field in pursuit of the ball. He caught it, arching up with his whole body and plucking it out of the sky. Lori felt something inside her chest swell, and her heart began to beat more quickly.

Just then, another boy who had been hanging around on the fringes of Perry's group came over to where they were tossing the ball. Lori recognized the roly-poly figure as Dave Carstairs, a junior who was always tagging after the senior boys with puppy dog adoration. It was obvious from the way he was gesturing that he wanted to join the game.

The senior boys just laughed and motioned for Dave to scram. Except Perry. Purposely ignoring his friends, he tossed the ball in Dave's direction. Dave fumbled a little as he caught it, then he broke out in a wide grin. He was in the game.

It was a small thing, but Lori couldn't help being touched by Perry's consideration of another person's feelings. He didn't seem at all like the same Perry who had humiliated her so terribly at Meredith's party. Was it possible she'd misjudged him before? Maybe he *was* as nice as he'd sounded on the phone that night. Four years was a long time. People could change. Hadn't she changed?

Suddenly, Lori regretted having turned Perry down when he asked her out. She still felt she'd had no choice, but she couldn't help thinking how closely Perry resembled the dream boy she'd always fantasized about—not just in looks, either.

Lori became aware that someone was pulling at her arm. She turned to find Kit smiling at her. "Hey, Lori . . . what're you daydreaming about this time? Don't tell me, let me guess." She held out an apple, waving one hand as if it were a crystal ball, "I see someone . . . yes, the mists are clearing . . . a boy . . . tall, dark, and handsome. You will fall madly, passionately in love and . . ."

Kit was interrupted when Alex seized the apple and took a gigantic bite out of it. Then the four of them dissolved into giggles. But even though the others had obviously taken Kit's prophecy as a joke, Lori couldn't help feeling a sense of anticipation. Maybe there was more truth in it than any of them knew.

Chapter Seven

Fifth period, Lori had gym. It was her worst class. Unlike Alex, she didn't have an athletic bone in her body. Not that she didn't try; it was just that usually when she did, she ended up falling flat on her face.

Miss Gordon, her gym teacher, had told her that her problem was a lack of confidence. When catching a softball, she invariably hesitated too long, afraid she was going to fumble it, with the result that she usually did. In basketball, she always aimed too low, and in tennis, too high. Once, in the seventh grade, she'd run the fifty-yard dash and was the slowest girl in the whole class!

A lot of it, Lori knew, had to do with having been fat. At her old school, she could never keep up with the other kids no matter how red-faced and sweaty she got from trying. Sometimes they teased her, making her feel even more self-conscious. Once, in the seventh grade, when the captains were choosing up teams for basketball, she'd overheard them whispering about her.

"You take her—it's your turn."

"Uh-uh. I had her last time. It's *your* turn."

Lori had wanted to cry. All during the game, her stomach had hurt from holding her tears in, and at the end she'd had to go to the nurse's office and lie down.

But the worst part of gym, in Lori's opinion, had been the locker room. She'd hated having to change in front of everyone. She was sure all her classmates were looking at her—noticing each roll of fat, counting each dimple on her thighs. She would always turn her back when she took her clothes off, doing so as quickly as possible. She never took showers with the other girls, either. She always waited until the end of the period, when everyone was gone.

Now, even though she wasn't fat anymore, even though no one ever made fun of her, and the worst grade she ever got was a C+, all those painful memories came flooding back the instant she laid eyes on the new girl, who had been assigned the locker next to hers.

Miss Gordon brought her in at the beginning of the period while they were in the midst of changing.

"Girls," she announced in a loud voice, "this is Gayle Rodgers! She's our new transfer student. I *know* you'll all make her feel welcome."

She made it very plain by her tone that she *expected* them to treat Gayle nicely *or else.* Miss Gordon was like that. She reminded Lori more of a drill sergeant than a gym teacher. She was tall and stringy, with short-cropped hair. She was so thin that her hips, waist, and chest looked exactly the same.

Gayle Rodgers was built the opposite—round as a pumpkin. She had curly red hair, not the orange-ish color most people call red, but a dark russet-red—the color of autumn leaves. Lori thought she probably would've had a pretty face, too, if it weren't so round. Gayle's cheeks were flushed as she stood beside Miss Gordon, looking as if she wanted to shrivel up with embarrassment.

Lori's heart immediately went out to Gayle—especially when several girls behind her groaned under their breath. She heard Marcia Connors mutter, "Boy, talk about Moby Dick! I don't want to be anywhere near *her* when we jump in the pool!"

Today was Swimming. Lori remembered that they would all be wearing bathing suits, and she felt sorrier for Gayle than ever. At the same time, she couldn't bring herself to welcome Gayle, other than a quick smile, when she came over and started getting undressed.

In fact, Lori desperately wished Gayle had been assigned some other locker. She couldn't bear being so near the new girl—it reminded her too much of the time when she'd been fat herself. Because she'd worked so hard to wipe out the memory, she didn't like even being *near* someone else who was fat. Deep down, she was afraid it might rub off like some contagious disease. She knew it was irrational, but she couldn't help it.

At the same time, Lori couldn't help being ashamed of the way she was ignoring Gayle. She knew what the first day in a new school was like. Not long ago she'd been in the same situation, and it had been a scary time for her, too. She would never forget how alone she'd felt during her first few days at Glenwood.

With a twinge of guilt, she turned her back to Gayle so she wouldn't have to be reminded anymore. Silently, she slipped into the shapeless black tank suit she'd been issued at the beginning of the period. She noticed, as she walked outside to the pool, how Gayle hung back from the others, and how, on her, the swimsuit that was so baggy on everyone else was stretched skin-tight.

Everyone in the class spent the first five minutes of the period doing butterfly kicks at the edge of the pool to warm up. The custodian had forgotten to put on the pool heat, so the water was colder than usual. Lori shivered as she clung to the edge of the pool, kicking up a froth.

Beside her was Nancy Colton, a girl who hung out with Marcia. Nancy looked over at Gayle and snickered, "I wonder if all that blubber keeps her warm."

Lori didn't say anything. She just kicked harder. She hated it when girls like Marcia and Nancy acted so superior! How would *they* like it if they were hideously disfigured in some accident someday, and people went around making nasty comments about them behind their backs?

Lori tried her best to look graceful as she swam her laps. Even Miss Gordon commented on her style, saying her breaststroke had really improved. She didn't say anything when Gayle swam clumsily across to the other side, except to give her a few pointers.

Five minutes before the end of the period, Miss Gordon blew her whistle. Lori joined in the mad dash for the edge, hoisting herself easily up onto the sun-warmed pavement surrounding the pool. She looked back over her shoulder and saw that Gayle was attempting to do the same, only she wasn't having much luck. Not wanting to draw attention to herself by swimming around to the end of the pool and climbing up the ladder alone, she was self-consciously struggling to haul herself up. Each time she was on the verge of rolling herself over the edge, her weight pulled her back into the water with a dismal splash.

Lori's first impulse was to lend her a hand, but she hesitated. Part of her ached with sympathy for Gayle's plight. Part of her wanted to run in the other direction as fast as possible.

While Lori struggled with herself Gayle finally managed to hoist herself up. She rolled onto the pavement with a wet, squelching sound. Several girls who were watching giggled softly. Lori saw that Gayle was close to tears as she trudged slowly back to the locker room.

A wave of shame washed over Lori. She could so easily have helped. Or, the very least, she could have offered a word of kindness to make Gayle feel better. What was wrong with her?

For the first time, she wondered if, in losing her

fat, she'd lost something else as well—something valuable.

"Eggs and butter. And a pound of hamburger, but not the expensive kind. Better get chuck." Old Mrs. Kornfeld pursed her lips as she leaned forward in her wheelchair. "And don't let that old pirate behind the butcher case charge you too much, either."

"I won't, Mrs. Kornfeld," Lori promised, stifling a smile.

She knew how frustrated Mrs. Kornfeld had felt ever since she'd broken her hip last month, so she didn't allow herself to get annoyed when the elderly woman became irritable from time to time. For someone as active as she'd been—even at seventy-five—being stuck in a wheelchair was a bitter experience.

Mrs. Kornfeld lived down the street from Lori and her mother. Before she'd broken her hip, she'd spent most of her time outdoors in her garden. That's how Lori had gotten to know her. On her way home from school, Lori had often stopped to chat. Mrs. Kornfeld was full of valuable gardening tips, and she usually sent Lori off with a paper bag full of bulbs or cuttings from her garden.

After Lori learned that Mrs. Kornfeld would be confined to a wheelchair for the next few months, she felt so sorry for her, she stopped by and volunteered to help out in any way she could.

What her offer had boiled down to was that one day a week she ran errands for Mrs. Kornfeld after school. She did a little grocery shopping, or picked up a book at the library. She really didn't mind . . . even when Mrs. Kornfeld became difficult.

"And don't forget the bread," Mrs. Kornfeld added. "Not that spongy stuff they call bread, either. I want *real* bread—the kind you can sink your teeth into."

"I won't forget," Lori said, tucking the list into the back pocket of her jeans. "I'd better go, Mrs. Kornfeld. I have to be back before dinner."

A smile crept into the corners of the old woman's down-turned mouth. She pushed a wisp of white hair from her forehead. "You young people never stand still. Always rushing off somewhere. I suppose you're rushing off to meet some boy, huh?"

Lori headed for the door, in a sudden hurry to get away. "I'll be right back. It won't take long."

Outside, she picked up her bike where she'd left it beside the lilac hedge that bordered Mrs. Kornfeld's property. Five minutes later, she cruised to a stop in front of Pearson's Grocery. She locked her bike onto the rack outside. There was only one other bike besides hers—a bright metallic-green ten-speed.

Lori liked Pearson's, with it's rustic atmosphere and uneven wooden floors. It always smelled like cider inside, probably because of the apples stored in wooden barrels in the back. She quickly gathered the items on her list, then angled her cart into line at the cash register behind a young mother with three children who were using their cart as a jungle gym. Lori smiled at one of them—a tow-headed boy of about three—when he peered up at her, his mouth smeared with chocolate.

Suddenly, she remembered Mrs. Kornfeld's chocolate addiction. She'd meant to get her some, out of her own pocket, as a treat.

Lori was posed to make a U-turn with her cart when a male voice behind her said, "Forget something?"

With a shock, Lori turned to find Perry standing behind her, his blue eyes directed at her like laser beams. He was holding a carton of milk. Oh, no . . . what was he doing here? Why was it she seemed to run into him wherever she went?

"I . . . it was nothing," she stammered, too embarrassed to sidle past him now.

"Listen, whatever it is, I could get it while you're checking out. Just hold my place until I get back." He smiled, sending a flutter of nervousness through her. "It's no trouble, really."

Lori was disarmed by his kindness, in spite of herself. "You don't have to," she said, a shy smile creeping across her face. "I just remembered, the thing I was going to get, she—the lady I shop for—she already has some at home." She told him about Mrs. Kornfeld, and how she sometimes ran errands for her. She tried not to make it sound as if it were a big deal, like she was doing Mrs. Kornfeld some enormous favor, afraid that Perry would think she was trying to impress him.

But Perry was impressed anyway. "I think it's nice what you're doing," he said. "A lot of people just don't bother. Or they figure it's someone else's responsibility."

Lori was reluctantly drawn into the circle of warmth that seemed to surround Perry. She forgot her shyness for the moment.

"I don't mind," she said. "Besides, it's really not that far out of my way."

"Do you live in the neighborhood?" Perry asked.

"Uh . . . sort of. I live about four or five blocks from here. On Cypress."

It was Lori's turn at the checkout counter. As she fumbled with her groceries, unloading them from the basket onto the counter, a head of lettuce slipped from her grasp. Perry caught it before it hit the floor. He handed it back to her with a smile.

"Thanks," Lori muttered, her skin igniting where their fingers touched.

"I guess this means we're neighbors," Perry said, his blue eyes riveted to her. "I live on Redwood Street." Lori noticed he was wearing a pair of bleached-out jeans and a blue chambray work shirt with the sleeves rolled up over his muscular forearms. A pair of sunglasses was propped on top of his head, and his brown hair looked windblown.

The jangle of the cash register broke through her trance. Lori dropped her gaze, fumbling in her purse for the money Mrs. Kornfeld had given her. Her heart was pounding so loudly, she was sure everyone in the store could hear it.

"Need any help with that?" Perry asked, catching up with her moments later as she was carrying her bag outside.

"No, thanks," Lori said breathlessly. "I have a basket on my bike. I can manage." Suddenly, she couldn't wait to escape. She felt so confused around Perry. On the one hand, she wanted to stand there and talk to him, but on the other, she felt so strangely uncomfortable that all she could think of was how to get away. Being near him created a storm of conflicting emotions she wasn't ready to deal with.

It turned out that the metallic-green ten-speed parked beside hers belonged to Perry. They both bent down at once to open their locks, their hands accidentally brushing.

"Sorry," Perry muttered. He smiled at her, his blue eyes crinkling at the corners.

Lori felt hot where he'd touched her. Suddenly she was all thumbs. It was a full minute of fiddling with the lock to get it open instead of the few seconds it usually took.

Lori mounted her bike, arranging her groceries in the basket. She looked over at Perry, who was straddled on his own bike, watching her.

"Well . . . I guess I'd better be going," she said.

"Me, too."

Still, they hesitated. For Lori, the moment seemed to hang suspended, outside of time. They just stood there, staring at each other. Lori was aware of him with every nerve of her body. She was filled with a slow, swirling warmth, from the roots of her hair to her peach-frosted toenails.

Then, as if in slow motion, Perry raised his hand. "I guess I'll see you in class," he said, his voice oddly thick. "Bye."

"Bye."

As Lori watched him take off down the street, the breeze raking his hair back, his broad muscular back hunched over the handlebars, she felt strangely empty.

Chapter Eight

Lori held up both blouses in front of the mirror. The red or the blue? Which one would go best with her new paisley skirt? Eeeny-meeny, miney-mo . . .

She tried to imagine she was seeing herself for the first time—as Shandra would be. Did she look sophisticated enough? Had she put on too much makeup? Not enough? Should she go for the natural look instead, so it wouldn't seem as if she were trying too hard?

Lori struck a modeling stance pretending that she was posing for photographers from *Seventeen*. She threw her head back so that her shiny blond hair rippled down her back. She planted one hand on her thrust-out hip; the other one she held poised in midair as if she were accepting some invisible offering.

"Diamonds again? Oh, John, you *shouldn't* have!" she cried, affecting a stagey voice.

Dressed only in her bra and half-slip, she pictured herself wearing a long, slinky evening gown, shimmering with sequins. She smiled, then the smile turned into a giggle. Well, maybe that was going a little too far. Sequins and diamonds weren't really her style, anyway. But she certainly could imagine herself modeling, say, a crisp white tennis dress or the latest fashions from Esprit.

She knew one thing for sure, though. At the end of today's seminar, she was going to go up and introduce herself to Shandra Britton—no matter what. No matter how embarrassed or awkward she felt. She knew that if she chickened out on this, as she had with the saleswoman at the Emporium, then she'd might as well give up her dream of becoming a model.

"Hurry up, Lori!" her mother called from the kitchen. "I have a hearing at eight thirty. Judge Bream will hang me by the thumbs if I'm late!"

"Coming!" Lori called back.

She quickly slipped into her skirt and tugged the blue blouse over her head. It was too late to go through her closet again. On impulse, she grabbed a purple scarf from her drawer and knotted it about her waist as well.

Lori paused in front of the mirror for a final inspection, before dashing out to join her mother. She gave her reflection a tentative, hopeful smile. Well, maybe she didn't look too bad. Maybe things would work out after all.

"Modeling isn't as easy as some of you might like to think. Mostly, it's a lot of hard work, and, believe me, even this glamorous profession has its share of disappointments as well."

Shandra Britton spoke before the audience of girls that had gathered for her seminar. So many had signed up that, while most of the other seminars were being held in classrooms, Shandra's had the whole Multi-Purpose room.

Lori stared at her, enraptured. She was a tall, willowy woman with reddish-brown hair she wore scooped up on top of her head. She looked exactly like she did in all those photographs, Lori marveled. She was around forty but still as glamorous as ever. And those bones! She had bones sticking out absolutely everywhere—from her high, curving cheekbones to the sharp blades of her hip bones showing through the straight, tailored skirt she was wearing. Lori was so envious, she sucked her stomach in harder than ever.

"Of course, modeling *does* have its rewards," Shandra went on. "A top model can make two hundred dollars an hour and up."

"Wow, that's more than I make in a whole year of baby-sitting!" whispered the girl seated beside Lori.

"Most models don't make that much, though," Shandra quickly added. "Also, modeling is a lot less glamorous than you'd imagine. For each photograph you see in a magazine, a model may spend hours and hours posing under hot lights . . . or sometimes out in the freezing cold. She can get cramped muscles from standing or sitting too long in one position, and sometimes the photographer can be overly demanding and insensitive to her feelings." Standing up on the stage, in front of a podium, Shandra smiled. She leaned closer to the microphone. "I'll never forget the time I posed outdoors for a bathing suit layout. It was the middle of winter, and I had to look as if I were enjoying every minute!"

After she'd finished giving her talk, Shandra said they could ask questions. A short, plump girl in the front row raised her hand. Lori recognized Roberta Friedman, from her history class.

"How do you stay so skinny?" Roberta wanted to know.

Shandra laughed. "Exercise, mostly. I spend a lot of time pushing my chair back from the table."

A wave of appreciative laughter rippled through the audience. Lori wondered if Shandra had ever been fat. It didn't seem very likely, but the thought was a comforting one somehow.

"Do you get to keep any of the clothes you model?" asked Roseanne Parker. Roseanne was one of the cheerleaders. She also came from a rich family and hardly ever wore the same outfit twice, Lori had noticed.

"Sometimes, but not very often," Shandra said. "A lot of times, the clothes a model wears are not even the right size and have to be held together in back with pins. All the years I spent modeling, I felt like a pincushion."

More laughter broke out. Lori could see that Shandra was doing her best to discourage all those who were only interested in becoming a model because of how glamorous it looked on the surface.

But she already knew what hard work it was. She'd read as many books on the subject as she could get her hands on, and she'd even heard Cheryl Tiegs talk about it once on the *Tonight* show. Lori wasn't afraid of a little hard work. The only thing she feared was not being considered good enough.

After the question-and-answer period, Shandra thanked them for coming and being so attentive. Everyone filed out, but Lori hung back, waiting for the auditorium to clear before she could get up the nerve to approach Shandra. There was still a group of girls flocked around her, asking questions. Lori waited until the last one was gone, then she stepped forward.

Shandra was busy gathering up the material she'd brought along to illustrate her lecture. As she struggled with a large portfolio of photographs, Lori reached out, eager to help.

"I'll carry that for you," she said.

"Thanks, I could use a hand," Shandra said, smoothing back a wisp of auburn hair from her smooth forehead. "It's not far. I'm parked just outside."

There was a faculty lot just above the auditorium. Lori carried the portfolio over to the car Shandra pointed out—a powder-blue Mercedes. She stood patiently while Shandra fumbled with the keys to open the trunk. She would have waited forever. It was worth it, just for the chance to be alone with Shandra.

After everything was tucked away neatly inside the trunk, Shandra straightened. "Now, is there anything I can do for *you?*" she asked, smiling.

Lori could feel herself starting to blush. Her throat felt very dry. She'd prepared a whole speech, but she couldn't remember a single word of it at this moment.

"I . . . well, actually, I was wondering if . . ." Lori stammered.

Shandra's smile widened, showing her perfect white teeth. "You want to become a model, is that right?" she supplied, as if she'd heard it a million times before.

Lori nodded, feeling more uncomfortable than ever. "Do you think . . . I mean, is there a chance I could be?"

Shandra pursed her lips slightly as she stepped back to give Lori a long, assessing look. Lori fought the urge to squirm out from under that cool, professional gaze.

"Well," Shandra said at last, "you certainly have the face. But a lot of it depends on poise, too. And, of course, you'd have to lose some weight. Not much—just a few pounds. The camera adds about twenty pounds to what's really there. . . ."

But Lori didn't hear the rest. Her mind was stuck, like a phonograph needle, on those few words: "*You'd have to lose some weight* . . ."

Shandra thought she was too fat to be a model!

Humiliation washed over Lori in a hot wave. She wanted to run away. Instead, she just stood there, pretending to listen with a stupid, phony smile pasted into place. How could she ever have been so dumb as to think she could measure up to Shandra's high standards?

Shandra dug into her tote bag and handed Lori a sheet of paper that listed some of the modeling schools in the area. "Good luck!" she called out cheerily, as she ducked into the driver's seat of her Mercedes.

"Thanks," Lori managed, though her throat was so tight, she could barely force the word out.

As soon as Shandra's car was out of sight, Lori crumpled up the sheet of paper and jammed it into her purse. What was the point of bothering with modeling schools now? She was too fat. She would probably always be too fat, no matter how much she dieted! Hadn't Shandra said as much to her face?

Lori walked slowly to her locker. The corridors were full of people dashing here and there and talking excitedly about the seminars they'd been to. She hoped she didn't run into anyone she knew. She didn't feel like talking. She just wanted to be alone.

She decided she would skip the next seminar, the one on social work. She couldn't bear staying in school a moment longer. She thought of calling up her mother and telling her she was sick. What was one more lie after all the lies she'd told? Then she remembered that Beth was going to be in court all day long.

After putting her notebook away in her locker, Lori set out for home on foot. She was too depressed even to care how many calories she was burning up by walking. What difference did it make anyway?

She would always be fat, if she lived to be a hundred! Fat, fat, fat. She would never be a model.

She would never be anything at all. Not a dancer, like Kit. Or a mathematician like Elaine. Or an athlete like Alex.

On her way through town, Lori passed by Robinson's Bakery. A delicious aroma of warm gingerbread wafted out the open door. Lori was tempted to go in. What was the use of constantly dieting when she was still fat? She'd might as well get some enjoyment from life, at least.

But some deeper instinct made her resist the urge. She hurried past. Maybe it had something to do with her father and how he'd failed her. In a way, it was the same with her mother. Beth was so busy with her causes, she didn't have much time for the most pathetic cause of all—her own daughter.

If I let myself down, Lori thought, who will I have left?

Chapter Nine

Lori dug her fingers into the warm, gritty earth. She grabbed the dandelion by its ropelike root, yanking hard until it came loose. The sun was hot against her shoulders and the top of her head, but she hardly noticed.

Beside her was the flat of plants she'd picked up at the nursery on her way home from school. Gently she pried a tiny marigold plant from its plastic container. Careful not to let the dirt from its root ball shake loose, she transferred it to the hole left by the dandelion. When it was filled in, she patted the earth around it.

One of the reasons Lori loved gardening so much was the feeling of permanence it gave her—of things rooted solidly in one place. She liked looking at the things she'd planted in the garden around her house, knowing that no matter how many shifts there were in her own life, she could always count on her flowers.

Lori straightened, brushing the dirt from the knees of her jeans. She gazed out over the carefully tended beds of marigolds and petunias, roses and gladiolus. Against the side of the house, where it was shady, she'd planted orchid bushes and ferns. Hanging from the redwood lath over the porch were ferns in pots, rose-colored begonias, and impatiens. Once in a while, Beth helped with the gardening, but it wasn't often she had the time. Lori didn't mind. She didn't consider it work; it was more of a hobby.

Lori refused to think about Shandra. Every time she did, her stomach knotted up and there was a sour taste in her mouth. That's why she'd stopped at the nursery on the way home from school to buy these flowers. Usually, when something bad happened, she could make herself forget it for a while by immersing herself in her garden.

She didn't know how long she'd been out in the backyard; she'd lost all track of time. The backs of her arms prickled with sunburn. She figured it must be around five, though. She could hear Mr. Griswald's TV next door, and he never watched it before five, when *Family Feud* came on.

The phone rang in the kitchen. Lori thought it was probably Beth, calling to say she'd been held up in court and wouldn't be home for dinner. She didn't hurry to answer it.

But it wasn't Beth. It was her father.

"Lori, honey, is that you?" Her father had been born in Norfolk, Virginia, so his voice was soft around the edges even though he'd lost all trace of a southern accent.

Lori opened her mouth to say something, but no words would come out. She felt stunned, as if she'd been struck by a blow she hadn't seen coming. She'd known, of course, that he would call her sooner or later, and somehow she'd hoped she'd be ready for it when the time came. Well, she wasn't. Especially not today.

Why did he want to talk to her, anyway? Why did he have to come back into her life now? After all this time, she couldn't make herself believe it was because he cared for her. If he'd loved her, or Mom, he wouldn't have gone away in the first place. He would've quit drinking a long time ago.

"Lori?" he repeated, as if he thought he might have dialed the wrong number.

She was tempted to tell him he had dialed the wrong number, but she didn't. She took a deep breath. "It's me," she said.

"How are you? Oh, honey, you don't know how good it is to hear your voice!"

"I'm fine," she said, keeping her voice even.

"Well, I'm not doing so badly myself these days."

"I'm glad to hear that."

"Lori . . . I know what you must think of me. All this time, and not even one postcard. Believe me, honey, if I could've written, I would have. I just . . . well, I just couldn't."

Lori bit down against her lower lip. She didn't want to hear this. She didn't want to know how miserable this last year had been for him. Why didn't he ask what it had been like for *her?*

"It's kind of a long story, so I won't try to get into it over the phone," he continued painfully, "I was hoping . . ."

"You don't have to explain," Lori cut in. "It's okay. I've been pretty busy myself."

"Do you like your new school?"

"It's not new, Dad," she pointed out. "I've been going to Glenwood for over a year."

He was quiet for a moment. She was sure he'd gotten her meaning. Finally, he took a deep breath and said, "Yes, I see. Well, I guess it has been awhile. A lot's changed. For both of us."

"I'm in the Art Club at school," she said. "I do a lot of sketching and stuff. I'm thinking of becoming an artist." She didn't know why she'd made up that last part. Maybe it was because she didn't want him to think she didn't know which direction her life was going in.

"Hey, that's great! You always had talent, even when you were a baby." His enthusiasm seemed forced, awkward. "I remember there was one time when . . ."

Lori squeezed her eyes shut. *Don't, Daddy!* she cried silently. *I don't want to remember the good times. Don't you see? It can never be that way again.*

"Dad, I have to go," Lori interrupted, before he could get started reminiscing about something that she couldn't bear to remember. "I have to go somewhere. I'm already late."

"Sure, I understand. We can catch up on all that

some other time. Actually, that's why I called. I was thinking of driving down your way, and I was wondering when would be a good time for us to get together."

Lori flinched. "I don't know, Dad. I'm pretty busy right now." She tried to sound casual, but her heart was beating so hard, it made her voice unsteady.

"I was thinking maybe in a week or so . . ."

"I'm going to be tied up all next week. I have this term paper . . . I'll be spending most of my time at the library. It's kind of important."

"What about the week after that? You'll be on spring break, won't you?"

"Uh, yeah, but Mom and I were planning to go away," she quickly lied. She was trembling all over, and she willed herself not to start crying. "We're going to look at college campuses. I applied to Cal Poly and UCLA."

"I see." She could tell from the way he said it that he understood exactly what she was trying to say. "Well, I guess we'll just have to make it some other time then. Tell you what, why don't I give you my phone number here? I'm living in Monterey now. Next time you get a chance, why don't you call me?"

"I will," she said, knowing she'd just told the biggest lie of all.

After she hung up, she sank down weakly on a chair beside the kitchen table. She stared out the sliding glass door for a long time, watching the sun spear itself on Mr. Griswald's antenna and finally melt below the boxwood hedge. Well, you got what you wanted, she told herself. Her father wouldn't be bothering her again. She would never have to see him if she didn't want to. She could go back to pretending he was dead.

But if that was true—that she'd gotten what she wanted—then why did she feel so awful about it? Why did she have this ache inside that wouldn't go away?

There was a piece of yellow paper sticking out from underneath the telephone book on the sink. She saw it was a flyer advertising the new pizza parlor that had recently opened in their neighborhood.

"The cheesiest pizza ever!" she read. "Free delivery!"

Before she knew what she was doing, Lori was dialing the number printed in bold type at the bottom.

"I . . . I'd like a large pizza with everything on it," she said quickly into the phone before she lost her nerve. She gave her address.

God, why had she done that?

Why not? another voice inside her urged. *What more do you have to lose?*

Lori was in the midst of devouring her pizza when she heard someone knocking at the front door. She decided not to answer it. She knew it wasn't her mother because Beth had her own key. Anyway, she didn't feel like talking to anyone right now.

She lifted a dripping wedge of pizza to her mouth. It wasn't exactly hot, but she didn't care. All she cared about was stuffing her face. She took a gigantic bite. Tomato sauce dribbled down her chin, but she didn't bother to wipe it off.

She thought about her father. She imagined him

sitting alone somewhere, in some motel maybe. Tears welled up in her eyes. She blinked them back. She wondered if he felt as bad as she did at this moment.

The insistent knocking had stopped. Lori sat back in her chair at the kitchen table with a sigh of relief. A sudden rattling at the sliding glass door behind her caused her to jump. Three familiar faces peered through the glass at her—Kit, Elaine, and Alex.

What were they doing here? Then Lori remembered the pizza in front of her, and she was flooded with shame. It was too late to hide the evidence, though. She got up and unlocked the door. It was getting dark outside. Her friends crowded in.

"Jeez!" Alex cried in mock indignation. "Did you hear us at the front—" She stopped as her gaze fell upon the nearly half-eaten pizza on the table. "Hey, I didn't know you had company."

Lori was so embarrassed, she didn't know what to say. She felt her face growing warm. A lie formed itself on her lips even before she realized what she was saying.

"Oh, that," she said. "A bunch of kids from the Art Club stopped by. They just left a few minutes ago. They were starved, and there wasn't any food in the house, so we ordered a pizza. I was just cleaning up the mess."

But it was no use. Before she was halfway through the lie, the dam burst and she began to cry. She sank down in the chair, folding her arms in front of her on the table and burying her face in them. Great, heaving sobs racked her body, and she realized it was all coming unraveled, all her lies, and she couldn't seem to put it back together again.

She felt a hand against her shoulder. "Please, Lori, won't you tell us?" she heard Elaine say. "Whatever it is, we'll understand."

"What're friends for?" Kit said.

Lori lifted her head. She wiped her wet cheeks with the crumpled up napkin in front of her. When she blew her nose into it, she smelled pepperoni.

She took a huge, shaky breath. "Oh, what's the use! You might as well know the truth. Then you'll see what kind of person I am!"

It all came gushing out then. "My father isn't really dead," she told them. "I made that up. He and my mom are divorced."

"That's not so terrible," Kit said softly. "It happens to lots of parents. Look at mine."

Lori took a deep breath. "That's not all. He . . . he's an alcoholic. I haven't seen him in a whole year because he's been in some kind of clinic."

Kit's blue eyes flooded with sympathy. "Oh, Lori, I'm so sorry! How awful for you! But it's not your fault. You shouldn't feel ashamed."

"That's not all—it's not just my father," she confessed. "It's me, too. I'm not what you think."

"What do you mean?" asked Elaine, frowning in confusion.

"I. . . . I wasn't always this weight, you see. I used to be really"—she paused, nearly choking on the word—"fat."

In a funny way, despite how ashamed she felt, it was good letting it all out. Lori felt strangely light. All those horrible lies . . . in some ways they'd been more of a burden than her fat ever was.

No one said anything at first. Lori's friends looked stunned.

Finally, Alex said, "I always sensed there was something you didn't want us to know. But I never thought—"

"I was so ashamed!" Lori cried, "I just couldn't tell you."

"Why?" Elaine wanted to know. "I mean, it's not as if you murdered someone. Besides, I can't believe you were ever really overweight. What do you mean by 'fat'?"

"I'll show you, if you don't believe me," Lori said fervently. "I have a picture."

She ran into her room and yanked open the top drawer of her dresser. From underneath a pile of underwear, she unearthed a picture that had been taken of her two years ago, at her uncle's wedding. She took it out and showed it to her friends.

"Which one is you?" Kit asked, peering at the out-of-focus snapshot.

"The fat one in the middle," Lori confessed. She pointed at the fuzzy figure standing between two slender bridesmaids. "We all wore the same dress, only I had to make mine because the bridal shop didn't have a size that was big enough for me."

"I can't believe it," Alex said, shaking her head as she sat down in the chair opposite Lori's. "All this time, you kept it a secret. Why didn't you tell us?"

Lori hung her head. "I was afraid to. I . . . I was so sure you wouldn't want to be friends with me if you knew the truth. If you knew how unpopular I was at my last school . . . ."

She stared at the leftover pizza on the table. She was remembering how it had been then. Her only real friend was a girl named Sandra, who wore braces and had a terrible case of acne. Then, in her sophomore year, the braces came off and her acne magically cleared up. Boys began asking Sandra out on dates, and Robin Wilcox invited her to join the Glee Club. All the popular girls belonged to the Glee Club, and suddenly Sandra had a lot of new friends. Soon it seemed as though she didn't have much time for Lori anymore. Whenever Lori called to suggest they go to a movie, or shopping, Sandra was too busy. Lori was too proud to let her know how hurt she was, so she'd just stopped calling.

"I don't care if you were a purple hippopotamus with two heads at your last school!" Kit cried. "We love you for yourself, not because of how you look! Anyway, I think it's fantastic that you lost all that weight. It's something to be proud of, in my opinion."

Kit's wide blue eyes shone with indignation. Lori was overwhelmed with love for her friends. How could she ever have doubted their loyalty? Would she have looked down on any of them if she found out they'd once been fat?

"I get it," Elaine said. She had that look of someone who's been struck with a sudden brainstorm, Lori thought. "It all makes sense now. You and Perry. The reason you didn't want to go out with him was because he's from your old school, right? He remembers you from when you were overweight?"

"Not exactly," Lori confessed. "The trouble is, he

doesn't remember me. I even had a different name then, before my parents got divorced. I'm just afraid he will." She groaned. "You don't know what it's been like!"

"I just wish you'd told us," Alex chided gently. "Maybe we could have helped."

"I didn't think anyone could help," Lori said. "Besides, I . . . I was afraid if you knew the truth, you'd think less of me somehow."

"Just because you were a few pounds overweight?" Kit exclaimed. "What kind of friends do you think we are?"

"Besides," Elaine put in, peering closely at the snapshot on the table. "You weren't really all that fat. It was mostly in your head. I once read about this woman who was so fat she got stuck in the bathtub, and her husband had to call the fire department to get her out. Now *that's* fat! It looks to me like you were just a little on the chubby side."

Lori sighed. "All I know is, I *felt* like an elephant. I really hated myself."

"I went through a stage like that, when I first started developing," Kit said. "No one else in the fourth grade had bumps on their chest. I was so embarrassed I wanted to die. What made it worse was when the boys started noticing. I used to hunch over so I wouldn't stick out so much. My mother thought it was just bad posture and was always yelling at me to stand up straight."

"My problem was, I felt like a giraffe," Elaine said. "I was taller than almost all the boys, even in the eighth grade. At all the school dances no one would ask me to dance except this one kid, Ricky O'Neill, who liked me for some weird reason. You should have seen us. His head only came up as far as my chin! Once, I had this horrible thought—that the only reason he'd asked me to dance with him was so he could look down the front of my dress."

Lori giggled in spite of herself. "Do you really think he was?"

"I'll never know for sure," Elaine said. "But if he was, it wouldn't have done much good. There wasn't anything to see."

Alex spoke out from her perch on the edge of the kitchen counter. "Something like that happened to me once. I was wearing this low-cut dress to a dance, and I wanted to look sexy, so I stuffed my bra with Kleenex. Afterward, when I got home and looked in the mirror, I saw there was a piece of Kleenex sticking up, right in plain sight! Boy, was I embarrassed!"

Suddenly, Lori knew it was going to be okay. Her friends really did understand. Besides that, she could see that each of them had hated the way they'd looked at one time or another. She wasn't alone, even if she'd thought she was the only one who ever felt that way.

"I'm sorry I didn't tell you sooner," Lori said, warmed by her friends' caring attitudes. "I get that way when I'm depressed about something. All I want to do is hide out. When I was fat, I'd sometimes hole up in my room for an entire day. Sometimes," she confessed sheepishly, "I'd even take a whole cake in with me."

Elaine was staring down at the table. "Or a whole pizza?"

Lori blushed. "I lied about having company."

"I figured," she said. "What I want to know is what made you depressed enough to want to eat a whole pizza? Is it something to do with Perry?"

"Not exactly," Lori said. "That's part of it, though." She told them what had happened with Shandra, then about her father calling her up and wanting to see her.

"That's why we came over," Kit said. "We couldn't find you at school. We even asked the nurse if you'd gone home because you were sick or something. Nobody knew where you were."

"After what Shandra said, all I wanted to do was run away and hide for a while," Lori confessed. "I guess it was dumb, but that's how I felt."

"You shouldn't let the opinion of one person get you down," Alex said. Her dark eyes flashed with sympathy nevertheless. "I remember when I first started getting serious about diving, I had this one coach who didn't think I had much talent. But that only made me want to try even harder . . . to prove how wrong he was."

"Besides, I don't think Shandra was telling you to give up," Elaine pointed out. "It sounds to me as if she was just giving you a few pointers. I'm sure she didn't mean you were fat. How could she? There's not an ounce of fat on you! You're just not a living skeleton like most of those models you see in magazines."

To emphasize her point, Elaine seized a copy of *Seventeen* from the stack of mail on the sink which Lori hadn't sorted through yet.

"Uhgh!" she cried, pointing to a particularly

emaciated-looking girl in a bathing suit. "If I looked like that . . ." She stopped, giving in to a sheepish smile. "Well, the truth is, I sort of do look like that, and believe me, it's nothing I'm proud of. I really hate being skinny. Honestly, Lori, I wish I had your figure."

Lori started to cry again, only this time they were tears of relief and gratitude. Nobody in the world had friends like hers. They were the greatest!

"What about your father?" Alex asked gently. "You didn't tell us what happened when he called."

Lori blew her nose into the napkin again. "I . . . I told him I didn't want to see him."

"You were upset at the time," Kit said. "You didn't really mean it."

Lori shook her head, scooping her long hair back with her hand. "Yes I did. It's true. I never want to see him again." Her voice trembled as she spoke. "He didn't want to see me when I needed him. Why should I see him now that he needs *me?*"

"How do you know he didn't want to see you?" Elaine asked. "He's probably been dying to see you only he just didn't know how to handle the situation. Or maybe he was just too sick."

"I thought of all that," Lori said. "In the beginning. I was mad, but I kept making excuses for him. Then I began wondering if maybe he'd been killed in an auto accident or something. That's when I started pretending he was dead. Somehow . . . I don't know why . . . it seemed easier than admitting the truth—that he just didn't love me enough to want to see me."

Kit came over to her then and put her arm around

her shoulders. "I'm sure that's not true, Lori. Sometimes I think that about my father, too. When he moved back to Glenwood, I figured I'd be seeing a lot more of him. But the funny thing is, I feel farther apart from him in some ways than when he was living in L.A."

"Does it bother you?" Lori asked. She had wondered if Kit ever felt the same way about her father.

But Kit only shrugged. "Sometimes, yeah, it does. But I don't think it's because he doesn't love me. Everything's changed since he got married again. I don't feel all that comfortable being around Vi and her kids, so I don't go over there much. Daddy and I, we still care about each other . . . but it's different somehow. Love changes, I guess—even when you wish it would stand still."

There was a silence, and then Alex spoke. She looked thoughtful. "It's one thing to pretend your father is dead, but what if he really were?" Lori could tell by the way her dark eyes glittered with tears that she was thinking about her brother. Even though Alex didn't often show it, Lori knew she still hadn't gotten over his death. "When someone dies . . ." Her voice caught. She leaned across the table and gripped Lori's hand tightly. "It's so final. Nothing can ever be as bad as when a person you love dies. Give your father a second chance, Lori. Someday you may not be able to, and then you'll regret it."

Lori was deeply affected by Alex's words. But she felt torn. She still wasn't ready to forgive her father, even though she couldn't help wanting to see him. Life was so complicated. In a way it had been easier when she was fat, she reflected. At least then she could blame whatever happened to her on her weight. It was a convenient excuse, one that kept her from ever having to look any farther than her mirror. Now she would have to learn how to handle her disappointments in different ways. But it wasn't going to be easy.

Well, at least she would have the help of her friends, and that was something, wasn't it? Lori looked at them, full of gratitude.

"Thanks for understanding," she said. "I . . . I guess I should've known you wouldn't hate me if I told you the truth."

"How could we hate you?" Alex asked. "Look at everything you've done for us. I don't think I ever would've made it through that bad time after Noodle died if it hadn't been for your support."

"And what about the way you stuck by me when I thought I was pregnant?" Kit put in.

"Anyone else would've run in the other direction after the way I acted when I thought you and Rusty were seeing each other," Elaine said, reminding Lori of the time Elaine had suspected her of trying to steal away the boy she had a crush on. "*We're* the ones who should be grateful to you!"

Lori grinned. "In that case, there *is* one big favor I'd like to ask from you guys."

"Name it!" Alex said.

"Would you finish off this pizza for me so I don't get tempted to eat any more myself?"

Kit was the first to grab a slice. "It's a real strain, but I think I can manage it."

"Yeah, what're friends for?" Alex laughed, helping herself. "I mean, in a real crisis like this, if you can't depend on your friends, who can you depend on?"

Elaine seconded the motion by taking a huge bite out of the last remaining slice. "I thought you'd never ask," she muttered with her mouth full.

Suddenly, Lori felt better than she had in the past week. She didn't even care how many calories she'd consumed by eating half a pizza. Finding out she had friends who really cared about her was all that really mattered.

Chapter Ten

On Wednesday, Mrs. Wiseman sprang a surprise quiz. It wasn't a quiz, actually, but more of a long essay question. Everyone in the class was supposed to write about an incident that had "profoundly affected" his or her life in some way.

Lori stared at the blank piece of paper on her desk for the first ten minutes of the period, chewing on her pencil eraser. She couldn't think of anything to write about. Everything about her life seemed *too* personal. But, on the other hand, Mrs. Wiseman had promised that if she read anything aloud she wouldn't say who had written it.

In a burst of sudden feeling, Lori wrote down everything she could remember about how she'd felt when her father moved out. She didn't mention that he was an alcoholic, or anything; it was mostly about how awful she'd felt, and how she'd stayed in her room, refusing even to say good-bye to him.

The next day, to Lori's horror, Mrs. Wiseman chose her essay to read aloud in class. Even though her teacher kept her promise and didn't mention a name, Lori was in an agony of embarrassment. As Mrs. Wiseman read, she slouched down in her seat, playing with a loose thread on her blouse. She couldn't even bring herself to look at Elaine.

Afterward, the whole class talked about divorce and how it had affected some of their lives. Lori was surprised to learn that nearly half the kids in her class came from broken homes.

"My mother was the one who moved out when my parents got divorced," said Celia Bordon, a frizzy-haired girl who sat in front of Lori. "I guess she was having some kind of nervous breakdown or something. She said she couldn't deal with all the hassles anymore. At first it was hard for us, but now it's not so bad. After I saw *Kramer vs. Kramer*, I told my dad he sort of reminded me of Dustin Hoffman."

"What would he do if your mother decided to come back?" someone asked.

"Oh, he'd probably take her," Celia said with a shrug. "Nobody likes being stuck with all the work of being a parent—except in the movies."

Some kids laughed. Lori laughed too, not because it was funny, really, but because it was so truthful. What if Beth had decided to take her father back? Lori wasn't sure how she would feel about that.

She glanced over at Perry out of the corner of her eye. Just as she did so, Perry looked over at her. He smiled tentatively. Lori felt herself blushing. Suppose he thought she'd been staring at him the whole time! She concentrated on her open binder, doodling a small sketch of Kenny Porter's sneaker stuck out in the aisle next to her.

"I remember when my parents got divorced," said Stanley Templeton, a quiet, red-haired boy in the front row. "I thought it was pretty neat at first, because my dad was buying me all this stuff and taking me out to lunch all the time—until I found out it doesn't last. They only do that at first while they're still feeling guilty over the whole thing."

"Yeah, I know what that's like!" put in Buddy Kowalski. "My dad was like that. Only with him, it lasted until he met Jean. Now he's spending all his time out with *her* instead of me."

There were other similar stories. The period flew by faster than Lori had ever known it to before. At the end of it, she had realized something important: that she wasn't the only one who had problems. Far from it. Other kids had big problems, too—some of them had the same type of problems. All this time, she'd been hiding hers away, ashamed to tell anyone. Maybe if she had, she wouldn't have felt so alone. . . .

When the bell rang, Lori didn't hurry away as she usually did. She was arranging her books on top of her binder when she became aware of someone beside her. She looked up and saw Perry standing there.

She felt shy, but this time, for some reason, she

didn't feel like running away.

"Hi," she said. Her heart was pounding against her rib cage.

Perry was wearing baggy white cords and a light-blue T-shirt with a sailboat stenciled across the chest. He was smiling at her in that open way of his, his teeth white against his tanned features. The floor seemed to tilt under her feet as she gazed into his blue eyes.

"Hi," Perry said. "Okay if I walk with you?"

Lori nodded, reaching for the books on her desk. But Perry was already one step ahead of her. He snatched up her books before she could do so herself.

"It's like I told you once before," he explained with a small shrug, his grin widening, "I'm the old-fashioned type."

Lori caught Elaine's eye as they were leaving the classroom. Usually, she and Elaine walked together, but she could tell from the way Elaine was beaming that she didn't mind being left behind this time.

Out in the hallway, Lori was aware of nothing but Perry's presence beside her. She hardly even knew she was walking. It felt more as if she were floating.

"By the way," Perry said. "I liked your essay."

His words jolted Lori from her dreamy state. "My essay?" she echoed, her face growing warm.

"Sure. I could tell it was yours."

"You could? How?"

"Are you kidding? You should see yourself—the way you blush. It's a dead giveaway." Perry laughed.

Lori fought against the wave of self-consciousness that threatened to engulf her.

"Anyway," he went on, "what I wanted to say was—I thought it was nice. It showed a lot of emotion. It's good that you can open up that way. Sometimes I have trouble with that."

Lori had a hard time believing him. Perry seemed so confident. "You do? I thought I was the only one. I mean, that essay—I'm not really like that in person."

"A woman of mystery, huh?" he teased gently. "Is that why you're always running away whenever I come near you?"

Lori didn't know what to say. She wasn't ready to reveal all her secrets yet, even though she'd been feeling much better about herself since confiding in her friends. She was still embarrassed about having been fat, but she realized now that she didn't have to let it ruin her life.

"It wasn't you," Lori said. "It was just . . . well, I've had a lot on my mind lately. Anyway, I'm sorry. I guess it was pretty rude of me."

"I thought maybe it was because you had a boyfriend."

"No, that wasn't it."

Perry looked relieved. "Listen, could you meet me after school? We could go somewhere for a Coke." He glanced at his watch. "I've gotta run, or I'll be late."

He handed her books to her, his hands brushing her forearms, as he did so. An electric thrill shot through her.

"Don't tell me you have to baby-sit, either," he added. "You're only allowed to use that excuse twice. The third time, you have to say yes or you're out."

Lori laughed. "I guess I have no choice then."

"Meet me in front," he called over his shoulder as he was dashing off. "I'll wait by the flagpole."

When he was gone, Lori rubbed her arm where he'd brushed it with his hand. She could still feel the warm imprint of his touch. She felt slightly dizzy, too. She wasn't sure whether it was from happiness . . . . or pure terror.

"It's kind of dark in here," Perry said. He fumbled for his chair in the corner. "Do you come here a lot?"

"Not really," Lori said. "Only once before." She didn't want him to know that the reason she'd chosen Bigelow's was *because* it was dark. "We don't have to stay if you don't want to. We can go somewhere else."

Perry reached across the table and squeezed her hand. A flash of heat traveled up her arm.

"No, it's okay. I'll get used to it in a minute. There, see, I'm already used to it. At least I can read the menu. By the way, how hungry are you?"

"Not very," she said. Food was the last thing on her mind at this moment.

"Good." Perry grinned. "Because I have exactly eleven dollars and fifty-seven cents in my pocket. It's probably not too cool to admit a thing like that, but I figured I'd better warn you or we'll both be stuck doing dishes afterward."

Lori smiled back. Perry had a way about him that was so open and natural. She felt more relaxed with him than she'd ever felt with a boy before.

"I'll have a Diet Pepsi," Lori told the waitress when she came over to take their order.

Perry ordered a hamburger and some fried onion rings. Lori admired him for that, too. She'd never had the nerve to order onions on a date. She was afraid the boy would try to kiss her, and her breath would smell of onions.

"I feel guilty eating in front of you," he said when their orders arrived. "You sure you're not hungry?"

"I'm on a diet," Lori said.

Perry stared at her as if she were completely nuts. "What for? You don't look like you need to lose weight. But then, I always thought you were pretty—even when you weren't so skinny."

He said it so casually, as if he were talking about the color of her eyes . . . or a dress she'd worn once, that at first Lori wasn't sure she'd heard him right. Then it dawned on her: He knew! He'd known all along!

She sat there, pretending to be absorbed in peeling the paper from her straw. She didn't know what to say. She was glad, at least, that it was too dark for him to see how much she was blushing.

When she looked up, Perry was peering at her over his mound of fried onion rings. "Did I say something wrong?" he asked.

Lori shrugged, putting on a smile to hide her embarrassment. "It's just . . . well, I wasn't sure you remembered me from our old school."

"I didn't right at first," he admitted. Although it

was dark, his blue eyes shone with a clear intensity. A lock of hair dipped over his eyebrow like a comma. "I mean, your name was different and all . . . . and you'd lost some weight." He stopped, covering her hand with his large one. "Lori, what's wrong? You look . . . . I don't know . . . . like you're in pain or something."

She *was* in pain. Only it wasn't physical. "I was hoping you wouldn't remember!" she cried.

"Why?" He looked surprised.

"Because . . . . because I . . . ." She couldn't bring herself to say it—that horrible word: *fat*. "Well, you were so popular at Morgan Hill. And I was such a nobody. I didn't even think you'd noticed me."

"You weren't a nobody," Perry said quietly, tightening his hold over her fingers. "Maybe you thought so, but I didn't. I just figured you were the shy type, since you were so quiet and all."

Had he forgotten about Meredith's party? she wondered. Probably. It was such a long time ago, after all. Suddenly, Lori was so tired of it all—the endless lying, the secrets, the fear of discovery.

"Why don't you just say it?" she blurted out.

"What?"

"What you're thinking. That the reason I was a nobody was because I was fat."

Perry shrugged. "Come on, Lori. You weren't *that* fat. Just a little overweight. But you were still pretty. I would've liked to have gotten to know you then, too, but you always acted like you didn't want anyone to get near you."

"You don't mean that," she said, not daring to

believe that he was telling her the truth. "You're only saying that to make me feel better."

"Is that what you think? Look, Lori, I can see you have some kind of hang-up about fat, but that's *your* hang-up, not mine. I come from a big family . . ." he paused and then smiled. "Not big, like in a lot of us, just *big*. My mother is I guess what you'd call pleasantly plump, and both my sisters are pretty chubby, too. But they're great people. Being a little overweight doesn't make them any less terrific."

"Is that why you danced with me at Meredith's party?" she asked, "Because you thought I was a terrific person?"

"Wow, you have a good memory! That was a long time ago. It just so happens I have a pretty good memory myself. I remember that time we danced. I always wondered why you took off on me like that. I thought you were having a good time."

"I was," Lori confessed. Then she looked him right in the eye. "Until I overheard some of your friends talking about how they'd dared you into dancing with me."

Perry frowned, as if he were having trouble remembering that far. "That sounds like something Mike Hansen would've said. He was a real jerk—always kidding around, making fun of people. I never liked him, he was just someone who hung around with me. Yeah, now I remember. He did make some dumb crack about you. He even dared me to dance with you. And that got me thinking—I'd always wanted to talk to you, so I decided I finally would. It just took me awhile to get up the nerve."

Lori couldn't believe what she was hearing. "Really?" She bit her lip to keep from grinning. He'd actually *wanted* to dance with her! All this time, she'd thought . . . well, it didn't matter anymore what she thought. Obviously, she'd been wrong—about a lot of things.

Perry squeezed her hand. "You haven't changed that much Lori. It's mostly in your head. You were always pretty."

Lori gave in to the grin that was tugging at the corners of her mouth. "You're really crazy, you know that?"

"Yeah, I know. It's a good thing, too. If I hadn't been so crazy, I would've stopped chasing you a long time ago. I mean, how much rejection can one ego take? You were pretty tough on me, Lori."

"I wasn't being tough on you," she said, "I was being tough on myself. I guess because I couldn't like myself, I didn't see how anyone else could, either."

"Well, you were wrong. I happen to like you a lot." He stared at her across the table. "By the way, what're you doing Saturday night?"

"Nothing," Lori said.

Perry grinned before taking a huge bite out of his hamburger. Lori sipped her Pepsi. She was so happy, she thought she might explode. When they were finished eating, Perry caught her hand as they walked outside. She squinted, shading her eyes against the bright sunlight.

"How long have your parents been divorced?" Perry asked.

Holding hands, they crossed Glenwood Avenue. There was a huge spreading oak outside the library, with an old wooden bench underneath. Perry brushed off the leaves and acorns before they sat down.

"Since we moved to Glenwood," Lori said. "My father . . . well, I haven't seen him in a while."

"He must live pretty far away then."

"That's not really it." She felt strangely close to Perry, as if she could tell him anything. Maybe it was the mood, or maybe it had to do with the kind of person he was. Anyway, for the first time she wasn't afraid of telling a boy how she really felt. "My father's an alcoholic."

Perry didn't seem shocked. "That's rough. I know. My uncle is like that. Only he doesn't drink anymore. He joined Alcoholics Anonymous. When was the last time you saw your father?"

"About a year ago. I haven't seen him since he moved out."

"Wow." Perry was silent for a moment. "You sound like you're still pissed off at him—like you wrote in your essay."

Lori picked up an oak leaf. It's sharp needle-pointed edges bit into her palm as she crushed it in her hand. "I guess I am," she said. "I don't see why he had to go away. Did your uncle do that—leave his family?"

"No, but in a way, that's sort of what happened. He was so sick, he didn't even know they were there half the time."

"Sick?"

"Yeah, that's the thing about drinking too much.

It's not like you're really a bad person or anything. It's . . . well, it's a sickness. I used to be like you—I used to think it was pretty disgusting of my uncle to get so drunk. Then when my parents started trying to help him, I started finding out all kinds of things—like how alcoholism is really a disease, like having the measles or something. Except it's a lot worse, because people feel sorry for you when you have the measles, but they don't have much sympathy for you if you're an alcoholic."

"I guess I never really thought of it that way," Lori said softly. "Like a sickness. Is it something you can really get over, do you think?"

"I guess it depends on the individual. Since he started going to AA about two years ago, he doesn't drink anymore. He told me, though, that there are still times, when he's really down about something, when all he feels like doing is having a drink."

Lori wondered if her father still felt tempted that way, even though he'd stopped drinking. "I still don't know if I can handle seeing him," she said uncertainly. "At least . . . not yet. I don't know if I ever will."

Then Perry did something very surprising. He put his arm around her and kissed her. Right there in broad daylight. His lips were warm against hers and slightly parted. She could feel the tip of his tongue touching hers. A feeling of excitement raced through her, flooding her with warmth.

"Whatever you do," he said. "I have a feeling it'll be the right thing."

Chapter Eleven

Lori was surprised to find Beth home when she got back. Usually, her mother worked until six or seven. Beth was sitting on the couch with her shoes off and her feet tucked underneath her. She wasn't doing anything, just staring out the window in a funny, vacant way. Immediately, Lori sensed that something was wrong.

She sat down on the couch beside her mother. "Mom?"

Beth looked over, as if faintly surprised to find her sitting there. "Oh, hi, honey," she said in a soft, dreamy voice. "It's funny . . . I was just thinking about my own mother. We weren't very close, you know—even at the end when I went to live with her before she died."

Lori had no memory of Beth's mother. Grandma Woodhouse died before she was even born. Even so, she'd heard Beth talk about her so often, she felt as if she'd known her.

"I didn't know you weren't close," Lori replied.

Her mother sighed. "I always felt she didn't love me as much as your Aunt Sally. Maybe she did . . . maybe it was only my imagination. It doesn't matter. The point is, I never forgave her. Even at the end, when she said she loved me, I couldn't say it back. Now she's gone, and it's too late."

Lori put her head against Beth's shoulder. She hadn't done that since she was much younger, but now it felt right. She felt very close to her mother at this moment. "I told Dad I didn't want to see him," she said.

"I know," Beth said. "He called me today. He's back in the clinic. He had a . . . relapse. He wanted you to know . . . in case you changed your mind about seeing him, that he wouldn't be able to for a while."

Lori was flooded with a painful sadness. "How sick is he?"

"I don't know. All I know is, it happens sometimes when people like your father leave the hospital too soon. He wasn't ready to face certain things. Don't blame yourself, Lori. It's not your fault. These things are always a lot more complicated than you think."

But to Lori, it didn't seem complicated. It all

seemed terribly simple: She had to see him. She'd wanted to all along, deep down, but she just couldn't bring herself to admit it. Now it didn't matter if she had a right to be angry with him or not. All that mattered was that he was her father, and he needed her. She needed him, too.

"I want to see him," Lori said.

Beth smiled. "I thought that's what you'd say."

"I wanted to all along. I was just too mad at him. I think I was trying to get back at him for leaving us."

"I know."

Lori thought about what Perry had said. "But he didn't mean to hurt me, did he?"

"Oh, honey, your father loves you. He always has . . . in spite of his problems. But sometimes, when a person has too many problems, they can get in the way of his showing how much he cares."

"That's the way it was for me when I was fat. All I could think about was how miserable I was," Lori conceded. "I forgot that other people have problems, too. I guess there are a lot worse things than being fat."

Beth smiled. "I've been trying to tell you that all along. But I suppose you just had to find out for yourself."

Lori thought about Perry—how wrong she'd been about him. "I've been finding out a lot of things lately." She sighed. "Suddenly, everything's so complicated. Does it ever get any easier?"

Beth considered her daughter's question for a minute. Finally, she said, "No, I guess it doesn't. I guess that's why I'm not such a perfect mother, either." She smiled. "In case you haven't noticed, I'm not always around when you need me. I don't suppose that'll change. I never was cut out to spend my time planting gardens and baking cakes. But also—in case I haven't mentioned it lately—I love you. A whole lot."

"I know," Lori said. "I love you, too."

A warm, delicious smell wafted in from the kitchen. Lori inhaled deeply. "What's that? Smells like something's in the oven."

"Oh, that." Beth cast her a sheepish look. "Well, once in a while I *do* get the urge to bake a cake." She got up and went into the kitchen. A minute later, she called out to Lori, "You want a piece? It's banana nut."

Lori wandered into the kitchen, watching in semi-amusement while Beth struggled with the cake pan. Finally, she managed to pry the cake free, minus one or two chunks which had stuck to the bottom of the pan.

Lori got out the plates while her mother sliced the warm cake. Then they sat down at the table to eat it.

"Delicious," Lori pronounced after the first bite.

"Do you really think so?" Beth asked anxiously. "It's not too mushy? I think I might have put in too many bananas."

"It's perfect," Lori assured her. "The best I've ever tasted." She wasn't lying, either—even if it was a little on the mushy side.

"Do you want some more?" Beth asked when they were both finished.

"No thanks," Lori said. "I've had enough." She was surprised to realize it was true.

She wasn't even tempted.

Chapter Twelve

"How did it go with your father?" Perry asked.

They were at the drive-in, watching a movie. Lori had already forgotten the name of it; she wasn't even sure exactly what it was about, but that didn't matter. She was far more interested in Perry. A warm thrill chased through her as he tightened his arm about her shoulders, pulling her closer on the front seat of his car.

"Okay, I guess. I mean, I was glad I went to see him and all. But it wasn't like in the movies—with everybody crying and hugging each other. I brought him a banana-nut cake my mom baked."

"Was he glad to see you?"

"I think so. It was awkward at first, because we haven't seen each other in a while. He was surprised to see I'd lost so much weight. He looked pretty much the same, though."

"That's how it is with situations like that," Perry said. "You think it's going to be all one thing or the other—like all bad or all good. But it's usually something in-between."

"That's a good way of describing it." Lori snuggled closer, resting her cheek against his shoulder. "In-between. That's really how it was. But I *am* glad I went. I have a feeling it'll get better, too. We were both sort of embarrassed this time. It's hard talking to someone you know really well when you haven't seen them in a while. There are so many important things to say, but you don't end up saying them. You end up talking about things that don't really matter, like what the weather's like and how you did on your last English essay."

"Will he be able to leave the hospital soon, do you think?"

"I asked him that. He said he's not sure. It may be awhile yet. Last time, he left too soon . . . . before he was really ready. I think that's why he had to go back. But he told me that knowing I still wanted him in my life was going to make a big difference."

Lori recalled how good she'd felt then. She realized her mother had been right, that being angry at her father had hurt *her* as much as it had hurt him. Maybe their relationship would never be the same as it had before he moved away, but at least she and her father knew they still cared about each other. It was a beginning.

A lot of good things were just beginning, she thought. *Perry, for one.* Lori tilted her head to look at him. As their eyes met, she was flooded by a feeling of happiness and confidence she'd never felt before with any boy. She realized it was partly because she trusted Perry. She sensed he would never do anything to try and hurt her.

The other nice thing was that she no longer felt she had anything to hide. She realized the person she'd been hiding from was herself. She'd wanted so badly to erase the memory of the old fat Lori that she'd refused to accept the fact that the old Lori and the new Lori were still the same person inside. If people hadn't liked her very much before, she supposed a lot of it had to do with her own attitude. As Perry had said, she'd put a wall up around herself that no one could get over.

Perry nuzzled her cheek. "We're missing the good part," he said. "I've seen this movie before. This is where the guy kisses the girl, and she tells him she's not in love with his best friend—it's *him* she really loves."

"That's okay," Lori said, in no hurry to tear her attention away from Perry. "I've got a good imagination."

"I'll bet."

Perry's mouth skimmed lightly across her cheek. He kissed her, the way he'd kissed her in front of the library that day—gently but searchingly. Lori could feel herself beginning to melt inside. It was even better than she'd always imagined it to be in her fantasies. He held her so tightly, she could feel his sweater tickling her through the thin cotton blouse she wore.

Lori felt breathless; her head was spinning.

She pulled back slightly. "Maybe we should watch the movie," she said. "I have a feeling we could get pretty carried away if we keep this up." She tensed in anticipation of his reaction.

But Perry didn't seem angry or put-out the way some boys acted when she withdrew. "I think maybe you're right," he said, his voice slightly hoarse.

Lori relaxed. They sat back and watched the rest of the movie. Perry kept his arm around her shoulders the whole time. It was nice, being so close . . . without feeling rushed. She'd never been the type who jumped into things quickly. When she got her feet wet, it was one toe at a time. Perry seemed to understand that.

"You missed a good seminar," Perry told her, as he was driving home afterward. "I saw your name on the sign-up sheet for the seminar for social work. How come you skipped it?"

"I didn't know you were interested in social work," Lori commented, hedging his question.

He smiled. "You never asked."

"Are you thinking of going into it as a profession?"

"Yeah, I've thought about it. You see, I'm a Big Brother. I'd like you to meet my little brother sometime. He's a neat kid. His big thing is helping me work on my car. The kid's a genius at changing spark plugs."

It was something she could imagine Perry doing—taking time to help some little boy who probably didn't have a father. He was so giving.

"I don't know anything about cars," she replied, "but I'd like to meet him."

"You didn't answer my question. About why you weren't at the seminar."

Lori felt flustered. She was on the verge of inventing a lie, then she stopped herself. No more lies, she told herself firmly.

She told Perry the truth instead. "I was too upset to come," she confessed. "After what Shandra said, I felt like such a loser. I was really hoping . . . you see, I had this dream of becoming a model. . . ."

"So what's stopping you?" Perry asked. "You could become a model if you really wanted to. You can't expect someone else to do it for you, though. Sounds to me like you were expecting Shandra Britton to wave a magic wand over you, like some kind of fairy godmother."

Lori thought about it for a minute. She realized it was true. "I guess I was," she admitted, surprised again at Perry's perceptiveness.

"When I wanted to become a Big Brother, they said I was too young. But I kept bugging them, and finally they gave in. If you want something badly enough, you've gotta be willing to fight for it."

What Perry said made sense, Lori decided. She thought about how easy it had been to lose weight once she'd really made up her mind to do it.

"I guess I wasn't really sure I *could*," she said. "I wasn't sure I'd be good enough."

"Well, you'll never know until you try," he pointed out.

"Listen, my mother sometimes takes pictures of

girls who want to become models. If you'd like, I could ask her to take some of you."

Lori hesitated. Putting together a portfolio was a real commitment. Did she really want to go for it? To take a chance on herself? Was it really possible she could succeed?

Yes, she decided.

Perry was right. If you wanted something badly enough, anything was possible.

"Okay," she told Perry. She looked over at him and grinned. "Okay!"

Chapter Thirteen

"Line up, girls!" Miss Gordon barked, as Lori's gym class filed out to the tennis courts. "B-team people on the courts, A-team people over by the backboards!"

Lori took her place with the other members of the B team. Gayle Rodgers sidled in alongside her, carrying her racket in front of her like a shield. She wore a guarded expression, as if in the space of her first week at Glenwood High, she'd learned not to expect too much.

Miss Gordon took a quick head count, then yelled, "Okay, girls, you can choose your partners. We'll play singles today, doubles tomorrow."

There was a mad scramble as the pairing-up commenced. At least four girls clustered about

Marcia, vying for the honor of being chosen as her partner. Lori looked over and saw the desolate look on Gayle's round, pink face. Gayle must have realized that no one was going to choose her, at least not willingly.

Without stopping to think about it, Lori touched Gayle's arm. "Do you want to be my partner?"

Relief washed over Gayle's features. "Sure," she said. "I'm not very good, though."

"That's okay." Lori smiled reassuringly. "I'm not so great myself. I spend most of my time chasing balls."

"Me, too. I guess we'll get plenty of exercise, even if we don't get too many balls over the net."

As they walked over to the court at the far end, Lori asked, "How do you like Glenwood? I mean, what's your impression, so far?"

Gayle shrugged. She lowered her head, hooking her red hair behind her ear. "It's okay, I guess. When I lived in San Francisco, I went to an all-girls school. But when we moved, my father decided I'd get a more well-rounded education if I went to a coed school. What he means is—boys."

"Well, there's certainly no shortage of boys here at Glenwood," Lori said.

"Do you have a boyfriend?" Gayle asked.

Lori thought about Perry; he was taking her out this weekend, to the new disco that had opened up in Palo Alto. She grew warm in anticipation. "Yes," she said shyly.

"I wish I did." Gayle sighed. For a moment, she lost that guarded look she'd worn. As if realizing it, she darted an uncertain glance at Lori. "I'm sorry. I don't know why I told you that. It's just . . . well, you're being so nice and all. It's not easy making friends at a new school."

"I know," Lori said. "I only moved here last year myself."

"But you're not"—she blushed, lowering her voice—"well, you know, *fat,* the way I am."

"I used to be." The words were out, before Lori even realized she'd said them. But she wasn't sorry. What did she have to hide?

Gayle's eyes widened in surprise. "Really? Wow! How did you do it? How did you lose all that weight? You're so skinny now!"

Lori smiled. "Well, it's a long story. . . ."

And as the two girls talked and rallied, Lori felt better about herself than she had in a long, long time.

"I can't do it!" Lori wailed. "There's a million people out there. They'll all be watching me. What if I trip or something?"

Kit, Elaine, and Alex crowded about to reassure her. They were standing backstage at the Emporium fashion show, which was scheduled to begin at any moment.

"You're *not* going to stumble," Alex told her, as if by saying it she could make it so. "You'll do just fine. I know how you feel. I'm always terrified before I dive, but so far I've never landed in a belly flop."

Lori wished she had as much confidence in herself as her friends had in her. She was in an agony of pre-fashion—show jitters and was beginning to wonder if volunteering for the event had been such a good idea after all. Since she'd gotten up the courage to launch her modeling career, she was terrified of failing now, more than ever. This beginning could also be the end of her would-be career.

Kit grabbed the hairbrush that was on the makeshift dressing table, along with an array of mirrors and cosmetics. "Here, let me fix your hair," she said.

"Does it look all right?" Lori asked, a fresh wave of panic washing over her.

"It looks fine," Kit said. "I just have to *do* something. I'm nervous, too!"

Lori laughed shakily. "What do you have to be nervous about? *I'm* the one who's going to end up making a fool of myself in front of all those people."

"Osmosis," Elaine explained, reaching out to brush a speck of lint from Lori's collar. Lori was wearing a short red skirt with a matching overblouse in big red-and-white checks. It was one of several outfits she would be modeling that afternoon. "In other words, when someone you're close to is nervous, you can't help being nervous yourself."

In spite of her butterflies, however, Lori was aware of a slow excitement building inside her. Modeling was no longer a dream. It was becoming a reality! Yesterday, Perry's mother had taken a roll of pictures of her. As soon as the photos were developed, she would pick out the best ones to be blown up for her portfolio. Now, if she could just get through this fashion show without tripping, or fainting. . . .

Lori smiled at Elaine, noticing she was wearing her new blouse. "You could be in this fashion show yourself. That blouse really looks great on you."

It really did suit her perfectly, Lori thought. Its full contours softened her angularity, and the rose color brought out the natural blush of her complexion. She wore it tucked into jeans, with a burgundy-colored belt and matching low-heeled slingbacks. Lori had never seen Elaine look so stylish.

"Thanks to you," Elaine pointed out. "Don't forget who picked it out. Remember, Lori, if you ever get tired of modeling, you could have a great career in fashion designing."

Lori blushed at the unexpected compliment. "I'll keep it in mind."

Mrs. Pollard poked her head into the backstage dressing area, really just a big storeroom, where the half-dozen or so models who would be appearing in the fashion show were busy putting the final touches to their outfits.

"Last call, girls!" she chirped. "We'll be starting in exactly two minutes. Lori, don't forget, you're on first."

Lori gulped as she nodded. "I'm all set, Mrs. Pollard."

Alex squeezed her hand, whispering, "Knock 'em dead."

"Don't think about all those people," Kit advised. "Make believe it's just us. You know, like all those times we got dressed up and fooled around, pretending to be models."

"Except you really are a model now," Elaine added. "Cheryl Tiegs, move over!"

Through the slit in the curtain, Lori could see the crowd gathered on either side of the runway. In the midst of all those faces, she spotted one that sent her heart racing. Perry was sitting near the front. He looked so handsome! He was wearing a striped shirt and skinny leather tie, with a sky-blue blazer that matched his eyes. Lori knew he'd given up tickets to a football game to be here, and a sweet warmth filled her at the thought. He really did care about her! Well, the feeling was more than mutual. . . .

Suddenly, she became aware of Mrs. Pollard's voice announcing her entrance through the microphone. Lori steeled herself. Shoulders back. Chin up. Ignoring the butterflies kicking up a storm inside her, she took a step forward, emerging onto the runway. She blinked, momentarily blinded by the bright footlights that ringed the platform. She faltered slightly, then found her balance again.

Then she was sailing down the center of the runway, hardly even aware that she was walking. At the end, she executed a perfect model's pirouette—exactly the way she had when practicing in front of her mirror all those times.

Applause rippled through the audience, engulfing Lori like a warm wave. Happiness swelled inside her. She'd done it! Not only had she done it, but it had been easier than she'd ever dreamed. Now, she could believe it . . . what her friends had been telling her all along.

"Loribeth Roberts Woodhouse, you're going to make it!" she whispered to herself.

WINNERS

by Suzanne Rand

A great new mini-series from the publishers of *Sweet Dreams*.

Being seventeen can be great fun – as Stacy Harcourt, Gina Damone and Tess Belding discover as they enter their exciting senior year at Midvale High School. Apart from years of friendship, the popular trio share their main interests in common – an obsession with cheerleading in the elite school squad, and boys! For all three girls, the intricate gymnastic jumps and routines of their favourite hobby are the best things in their lives – but the gorgeous footballers they are supporting are definitely the icing on the cake! Picked to lead the cheering, the girls know they have one of the school's highest honours and a big responsibility to be the best that they can be in every way.

Each book highlights the story of one of the girls.

1. **THE GIRL MOST LIKELY**
2. **ALL AMERICAN GIRL**
3. **THE GOOD-LUCK GIRL**

WINNERS – available wherever Bantam paperbacks are sold!